Old Testament
Part One

Greg Kappas and Jared Nelms, EDS.

Old Testament Part One
Book Four in TTI's Foundational Curriculum

© 2012 by The Timothy Initiative

International Standard Book Number: 978-1477582640

All rights reserved. Published and Printed in the United States of America.

Library of Congress Cataloging-in-Publication Data

No part of this book covered by the copyrights heron may be reproduced or copied
in any form or by any means without written permission of the publisher.

Scripture quotations are from: The New King James Version
Copyright © 1979, 1980, 1982 by Thomas Nelson, Inc.
Used by permission. All rights reserved.

First Edition-North America
Second Edition

THE TIMOTHY INITIATIVE

"What you have heard from me in the presence of many witnesses entrust to faithful men who will be able to teach others also."

2 Timothy 2:2

Acknowledgements

TTI gives special gratitude to the Docent Group and the leadership of Glenn Lucke and Jared Wilson (Docent Executive Editor for this project). The Docent writer, Steve Wamberg (OT 1 and 2) demonstrated persistence on this project and we are thankful. TTI is very grateful for Rev. Jared Nelms and his extensive supplemental work on both Old Testament 1 and 2.

TTI also gives thanks to Dr. David Nelms, our Founder/President for his vision and influence to see this New Curriculum written. Dr. Nelms has lived humbly to see you succeed greatly in Jesus Christ.

We express our gratitude for the fine, long editorial labor to TTI Executive Editor and Director, Dr. Greg Kappas and the Executive Editorial Assistant and International Director, Rev. Jared Nelms. In addition we thank the entire TTI editorial team of Dr. David Nelms, Rev. Jesse Nelms, Rev. Larry Starkey, Rev. Lou Mancari and Dr. David Nichols. Each of you has given such remarkable grace to us and now to these church planters.

TTI is greatly appreciative of the Grace Fellowship elders, pastors, administrative staff, leaders and GF family. TTI was birthed out of this "church for all nations." Thank you for your generosity in launching this exponential network of church planting movements.

TTI's Board of Directors has given us freedom and focus to excel still more. We are deeply moved by these men and women of God. Our TTI investor base of financial and prayer partners extend around the globe. These individuals, churches, ministries, networks, corporations and organizations are essential and strategic to our collective health and Kingdom impact. Thank you!

We thank the TTI Continental Directors, Regional Directors, National Directors and District/Training Center Leaders for your ministry of love and commitment. You are the ones that forge into new and current frontiers with the Gospel. You truly are our heroes.

Finally, we are forever grateful to you, the church planter. You are planting an orchard, a church planting center through your local church that will touch your region and the world with the Gospel of Jesus Christ. We are honored to serve the Lord Jesus Christ and you. You will make a difference for our great God as you multiply healthy churches for His glory. We love you and believe in you!

TTI Staff Team
July 2010

This workbook is the fourth of 10 workbooks which assist in equipping church planting leaders to start churches that saturate a region and help reach every man, woman and child with the Good News of our Lord. Below, is the list of this initial Curriculum.

TTI Curriculum

Workbook Number/Course:

1. Hermeneutics
2. Homiletics
3. Church Planting (New Testament – Acts, Evangelism, Discipleship, Spiritual Life, T4T)
4. **Old Testament 1**
5. Old Testament 2
6. New Testament Gospels
7. New Testament Pastoral Epistles
8. New Testament General Letters
9. Major Bible Doctrines
10. Apologetics-Church History-Spiritual Warfare

Table of Contents

Introduction 8

Books of the Law

Chapter 1: Genesis 11

Chapter 2: Exodus 16

Chapter 3: Leviticus 21

Chapter 4: Numbers 25

Chapter 5: Deuteronomy 28

Books of History

Chapter 6: Joshua 31

Chapter 7: Judges 35

Chapter 8: Ruth 39

Chapter 9: 1 Samuel 42

Chapter 10: 2 Samuel 45

Chapter 11: 1 Kings 49

Chapter 12: 2 Kings 52

Chapter 13: 1 Chronicles 55

Chapter 14: 2 Chronicles 58

Chapter 15: Ezra 60

Chapter 16: Nehemiah 63

Chapter 17: Esther 66

Books of Poetry

Chapter 18: Job 69

Chapter 19: Psalms 72

Chapter 20: Proverbs 75

Chapter 21: Ecclesiastes 78

Chapter 22: Song of Solomon 81

Books of Prophecy

Chapter 23: Isaiah 84

Chapter 24: Jeremiah 87

Chapter 25: Lamentations 90

Chapter 26: Ezekiel 92

Chapter 27: Daniel 95

Chapter 28: Hosea 98

Chapter 29: Joel 101

Chapter 30: Amos 104

Chapter 31: Obadiah 107

Chapter 32: Jonah 109

Chapter 33: Micah 112

Chapter 34: Nahum 115

Chapter 35: Habakkuk 118

Chapter 36: Zephaniah 121

Chapter 37: Haggai 124

Chapter 38: Zechariah 127

Chapter 39: Malachi 130

Endnotes 134

NOTES

Introduction

Why Read the Old Testament in the 21st Century?

The Old Testament is a special collection of 39 books. It tells the story of God and His people, the Jews, before the time of Jesus Christ.

These books are often divided into four sections. The first section is the Law, which contains both the rules and earliest history of the Hebrew people. The second section has the History books that are the record of ancient Israel's rise and decline. The third section is Poetry. This section has songs of worship, collections of wise sayings, and a story of faith. The fourth section is the Prophets. It records God's message through the men He chose to reveal His blessings, judgments, and promises.[1]

Here are the books of the Old Testament as divided into these sections:

The Law	**History**	**Poetry**	**Prophets**
Genesis	Joshua	Job	Isaiah
Exodus	Judges	Psalms	Jeremiah
Leviticus	Ruth	Proverbs	Lamentations
Numbers	1 Samuel	Ecclesiastes	Ezekiel
Deuteronomy	2 Samuel	Song of Solomon	Daniel
	1 Kings		Hosea
	2 Kings		Joel
	1 Chronicles		Amos
	2 Chronicles		Obadiah
	Ezra		Jonah
	Nehemiah		Micah
	Esther		Nahum
			Habakkuk
			Zephaniah
			Haggai
			Zechariah
			Malachi

The Old Testament was written between 1440 BC and about 400 BC. Most is about the people and events of those times and before, and the work of God in their lives. Why should someone read the Old Testament today?

1. **Jesus taught the Old Testament is God's Word.** As a result, it has very important information about God and His will for us. In fact, the Old Testament was so important that Jesus said:

    Do not think that I came to destroy the Law or the Prophets [the Old Testament]. I did not come to destroy but to fulfill. For assuredly, I say to you, till heaven and earth pass away, one jot or one tittle will by no means pass from the law till all is fulfilled (Mat. 5:17-18).

- A "jot" is the smallest Hebrew letter. A "tittle" is a longer stroke of a Hebrew letter. Jesus would not change any part of the Old Testament; not even the details of how people had written it down.[2]
- The writers of the New Testament also had a deep respect for the Old Testament as God's Word. This is clear from the way they talked about the Old Testament as they wrote under the inspiration of the Holy Spirit:
    - ▶ The apostle Peter taught that the Holy Spirit was in the Old Testament writers. God guided those writers to testify about Jesus *(1 Pet. 1:10-11)*.
    - ▶ Peter again wrote that God inspired the Old Testament writers to prophesy about Jesus *(2 Pet. 1:21)*.
    - ▶ Paul said that all Scripture (including the Old Testament) was God-breathed *(2 Tim. 3:16)*.
    - ▶ The writer of Hebrews says God spoke to His people through the Old Testament prophets, just as He spoke to His people through Jesus *(Heb. 1:1-2)*.

It is clear that Jesus and the New Testament writers believed that the Old Testament carries God's message.

2. **We should read the Old Testament to learn more about how God laid the foundations of His world and our faith.** One of the most important verses in the whole Bible is the first. *Genesis 1:1* tells us, *"In the beginning, God created the heavens and earth."* All that we see, and all that we have, comes from God. How can He love us that much? What does He expect from us? The stories of the Old Testament help answer those questions. Watch for the many ways God showed His power to remind people that He is the Creator and Ruler. A few of those ways include:
    - The flood that swept away everyone but Noah and his family *(Gen. 7:1-8:19)*.
    - The destruction of Sodom and Gomorrah for their sin *(Gen. 19:1-21)*.
    - The plagues on Egypt for the Pharaoh's refusal to set Israel free *(Exo. 7:14–12:30)*.
    - The food God provided in the wilderness for Israel *(Exo. 16)*.
    - The fire God sent to destroy the altar of a false god *(1 Kin. 18:20–39)*.
    - Look for ways God provided for people to learn to walk more closely with Him.
    - God gave His <u>Law</u> so His people could live a life that pleased Him *(Lev. 20:22-24)*.
    - David often drew closer to God through <u>worship</u> *(Psa. 63:7-8, 28:6-7)*.
    - Daniel spent time in <u>prayer</u> to seek God's mercies and understand a king's dream. Daniel had to be very close to God to understand all of this correctly *(Dan. 2:14-23)*.

3. **Learn from the history of God's people.** When God's people were faithful, God blessed them. When they were not faithful, they suffered the results of their disobedience. Here are some examples:
    - When Israel turned away from God, their families fell apart *(Jer. 19:4-9)*.
    - When Israel chose to obey God, God brought them success *(Jos. 6)*.
    - What one person does can hurt or help a whole nation *(Jos. 7:10-26)*.

NOTES

As you learn the lessons of Old Testament history, you will see how they apply today. The results of obeying or disobeying God are much the same. What happens to families in nations today that reject God's ways? What difference can one person today make in a nation?

4. **As you read the Old Testament be sure to note God's promises, blessings and judgments.** Many of these are found in the words of the prophets. Some of the most exciting promises are the prophecies about Jesus Christ. These prophecies about the Messiah, Jesus, are just a few found in the Old Testament book of Isaiah:
   - He would be born of a virgin *(Isa. 7:14)*.
   - He would obey the Lord in His mission *(Isa. 50:4-9)*.
   - He would freely submit to suffering *(Isa. 50:6, 53:7-8)*.
   - He would take on Himself the sins of the world *(Isa. 53:4-6, 10-12)*.
   - He would triumph over death *(Isa. 53:10)*.[3]

Those prophecies are just the beginning. You will find many more as you explore the Old Testament. The Old Testament shows us how important it is to walk in the ways of God. That wisdom is just as important now as it was 3,000 years ago. The Old Testament:
   - Gives us story after story of people who learned to walk with God.
   - Gives us wisdom from the very heart of God.
   - Offers songs and poems that we can use to worship God today.
   - Makes it clear that obeying God is not always easy, but is required for those who follow God.
   - Points to the fulfilled promise we have in Jesus Christ.

May God bless you as you *"study to show yourself approved, rightly dividing the word of truth" (2 Tim. 2:15)*.

Chapter 1
Genesis

1. **Introduction and Title**

    A. Genesis is the first book in the five books of the Bible called the Pentateuch (Genesis, Exodus, Leviticus, Numbers, and Deuteronomy). "Pentateuch" means "five books." These books cover the time from Creation through the death of Moses around 1405 BC.
    - This section of the Bible is also called "the Law." "The Law" refers to the books written by Moses. These books contain the many laws God gave to His people through the prophet Moses. These laws cover almost every area of life. They are the basis of how God's people would understand right and wrong.
        - ▶ These books also describe the beginning of the world and the beginning of God's covenant people, Israel.
        - ▶ God is shown as the Creator of the universe, and the Creator of His people.[4]

    B. The title "Genesis" means "beginnings" or "source."

    C. Genesis talks about beginnings:
    - The Creation *(chapters 1, 2)*.
    - Sin – how sin entered the world *(3:1-24)*.
    - The peoples of the earth *(chapters 5, 10, 11)*.
    - The covenant between God and His people that started with Abraham *(12:1 – 14:24)*.

2. **Authorship and Date**

    A. Moses is the author of Genesis.
    - In the Bible, Moses is said to be the author of all five books of the Law *(Jos. 1:7; Dan. 9:11-13; Joh. 7:19; Rom. 10:19)*.

    B. Genesis, along with the rest of the books of the Law, was written sometime around 1402 BC.[5]

3. **Purpose, Themes & Structure**

    A. Genesis' purpose is to tell the history behind God's covenant with His chosen people, Israel.

    B. The themes of Genesis have to do with beginnings.
    - The beginning of the created world *(1:1-2:3)*.
    - The beginning of the human race *(2:4-25)*.
    - The beginning of the nations of earth *(10:1-11:32)*.
    - The beginning of the covenant between God and His people through Abraham *(chapters 11-50)*.

NOTES

- ▶ A covenant is an agreement between two parties that usually requires action from one or both parties.
- ▶ God put a covenant into action between Himself and Abraham. These were the everlasting promises that God said He would perform in His covenant with Abraham.
  - ▷ God would create a great nation through Abraham *(18:18)*.
  - ▷ God would bless Abraham with long life *(15:15)*, and prosperity *(13:2)*.
  - ▷ God would make Abraham's name live on after he died *(17:5)*.
  - ▷ Abraham would be a blessing to others *(12:8)*.
  - ▷ Those who blessed Abraham would be blessed *(12:3)*.
  - ▷ Those who cursed Abraham would be cursed *(12:3)*.
  - ▷ All the families of the earth would be blessed through Abraham *(12:3)*.
- ▶ The covenant with Abraham extended beyond his own life on to those who also followed God.
- ▶ God's covenant promises were unconditional. Yet God required obedience from Abraham so he and his family could receive the full blessings of the covenant.
  - ▷ Abram and Sarai had to leave their home for a new land *(12:1)*.
  - ▷ Abraham had to be a blessing to others *(12:2)*.
  - ▷ Abraham had to walk before God and be blameless *(17:1)*.
  - ▷ Abraham had to circumcise the males in his household as a covenant sign *(17:10)*.

C. Genesis is structured in two main parts.
  - History before the Covenant People *(1:1-11:9)*. These are the events leading up to God's covenant with Abraham.
    - ▶ God's creation of the universe *(1:1-2:25)*.
    - ▶ Adam and Eve's fall into sin *(3:1-24)*.
    - ▶ God's judgment through the Great Flood *(6:5-8:22)*.
    - ▶ God overcomes the pride of men at the Tower of Babel *(10:1-11:32)*.
  - History of the First Covenant People *(11:10-50:26)*. These are the stories of Abraham, Isaac, Jacob and Joseph.
    - ▶ These men are often called Israel's patriarchs. A "patriarch" is a founder of a family or tribe.[6]
    - ▶ Israel counted Abraham as its founder. His son Isaac and grandson Jacob followed through with possessing the land of Canaan because of God's covenant with Abraham *(see Deu. 1:8)*.
      - ▷ In the same way, Israel said the land of Canaan was theirs because of God's covenant with Abraham, Isaac and Jacob.
    - ▶ Although Joseph lived in Egypt as an adult, he still felt a strong connection with Canaan and asked to be buried there *(50: 24-25)*.
    - ▶ All four of these patriarchs believed God would continue His covenant with His people.

4. Historical Background

Genesis was written at a time (about the 15th century BC) when most people believed there was no single, true God above all others. Many people, especially in and around the ancient Middle East, believed in many gods with different degrees of power. What Genesis said about the power of the one true God, and that God was involved in human history, made its ideas unique.

5. Development of Message

Genesis introduces main sections of the book with a phrase "This is the history" or "These are the generations."
- There are 12 such places in Genesis.
  - ▶ Creation as a whole *(1:1-2:3)*.
  - ▶ The heavens and earth *(2:4-4:26)*.
  - ▶ The book of Adam *(5:1-6:8)*.
  - ▶ Noah *(6:9-9:29)*.
  - ▶ The sons of Noah *(10:1-11:9)*.
  - ▶ Shem, one son of Noah *(11:20-26)*.
  - ▶ Terah, the father of Abraham *(11:27-25:11)*.
  - ▶ Ishmael *(25:12-18)*.
  - ▶ Isaac *(25:19-35:29)*.
  - ▶ Esau *(36:1-8)*.
  - ▶ Esau, father of the Edomites *(36:9-37:1)*.
  - ▶ Jacob *(37:2-50:26)*.
- Notice that this list begins with a very broad focus of all creation and narrows its focus as it continues, ending on the people of the covenant.

6. Theology

A. Everything exists because of God *(1:1; see Act. 17:24-28)*.

B. God created man in His image *(1:26-28, 2:4-7)*.
- The image of God in man is not physical, because God is spirit *(Joh. 4:24)*. This means the image of God in mankind is moral, intellectual, and spiritual. In these ways, people are supposed to reflect God's character on earth.
- When God breathed into the first man, He breathed the moral, intellectual, relational and spiritual aspects of His life into mankind. These things make us completely different from the animals God created.

C. The fall of Adam and Eve opened the way for sin to control people *(3:1-24)*. Sin does this in two ways.[7]
- Through self-deception. This happens when, like Eve, we choose to believe a lie about God and His ways *(3:13)*.
- Through self-will. This happens when, like Adam, we choose to ignore God's authority and listen to our own desires *(3:17)*.

D. God rules over the universe. He has the power to bless and to curse according to man's obedience *(12:1-3)*.

E. God has made Himself known in both word and deed to Israel's ancestors *(chapters 11 – 50)*.
- The covenant between God and Abraham *(15:1-21)*, was continued through Isaac *(26:24)*, and Jacob *(26:3-5; 35:9-13)*.
- God took action to protect His covenant people (the people who descended from Abraham) in many ways. These include:
    ▶ Protecting Abraham and Sarah from destroying the opportunity to begin their family line *(12:10-20; 20:1-16)*.
    ▶ Protecting Isaac and Rebekah from the anger of Abimelech the Philistine *(26:6-13)*.
    ▶ Protecting Jacob from the anger of Esau *(33:4-11)*.
    ▶ Protecting Joseph from death at the hands of his brothers *(37:17-28)*.
    ▶ Putting Joseph in place in Egypt to give Israel food and care during a great famine *(47:1-6)*.

F. God has established Israel to bless the families of the earth *(35:9-13)*.

7. Uniqueness and How to Preach It in Your New Church Plant

Genesis shows that everything we see or do connects back to God, who created and sustains everything.
- Preach that God alone is the Ruler of the universe. Everything exists because of God. As Ruler, God expects people to obey Him. As our Creator, God loves and wants to bless people *(47:28-50:26)*.
- Preach that God is faithful to fulfill His promises. He will do what is necessary to keep His covenants *(16:1-22:19)*.

Assignment:

Look at the passages where God states His covenant with Abraham *(Gen. 15:1-21)*, and repeats it to Isaac *(Gen. 26:1-5, 24)*, and Jacob *(Gen. 26:3-5; 35:9-13)*. In the space below, list the covenant promises that are the same to all three men.

8. Outline of Genesis[8]

A. History before the Covenant People *(1:1-11:32)*.
- Creation *(1:1-2:3)*.
- Creation of man and woman *(2:4-25)*.
- Sin and the fall *(3:1-4:26)*.
- Family histories from Adam to Noah *(5:1-32)*.
- The Flood *(6:1-9:29)*.
- Early nations and the Tower of Babel *(10:1-11:32)*.

B. History of the Early Covenant People *(12:1-50:26)*.
- Abraham *(12:1-25:18)*.
  - Call and Covenant by Faith *(12:1-14:24)*.
  - Covenant confirmed *(15:1-17:27)*.
  - Lot delivered from Sodom *(18:1-19:38)*.
  - Abraham and Abimelech *(20:1-18)*.
  - Isaac, the son of promise *(21:1-24:67)*.
  - Abraham's last years *(25:1-18)*.
- Isaac *(25:19-26:35)*.
  - Esau and Jacob born *(25:19-28)*.
  - Esau sells birthright to Jacob *(25:29-34)*.
  - Isaac and Abimelech II *(26:1-16)*.
  - Argument over Beersheba *(26:17-33)*.
  - Esau's wives *(26:34-35)*.
- Jacob also named Israel *(27:1-37:1)*.
  - Early years *(27:1-46)*.
  - Exile and journey *(28:1-22)*.
  - Jacob and Laban *(29:1-33:15)*.
  - Jacob returns to the Promised Land *(33:16-35:20)*.
  - Families of Jacob and Esau *(35:21-37:1)*.
- Joseph *(37:2-50:26)*.
  - Early years of Joseph *(37:2-36)*.
  - Judah and Tamar *(38:1-30)*.
  - Joseph gains favor in Egypt *(39:1-41:57)*.
  - Joseph receives his brothers in Egypt *(42:1-45:15)*.
  - Joseph receives Jacob in Egypt *(45:16-47:26)*.
  - Jacob's last days *(47:27-50:14)*.
  - Assurance of forgiveness *(50:15-26)*.

> NOTES

Chapter 2
Exodus

1. Introduction and Title

A. Exodus continues the account of Genesis. It tells about the deliverance of Israel from slavery in Egypt. It also records Israel's beginnings as a nation, operating under God's laws and covenant during its wilderness journey towards the Promised Land.

B. "Exodus" is the Greek title of this book. It means "going out" or "exit."

C. Exodus is the second of the five books of the Law in the Old Testament. It is also includes one of the greatest stories of redemption in the Old Testament.

2. Authorship and Date

A. Moses is the author of Exodus.

B. Exodus was written between the time of the Exodus (beginning around 1446 BC) and the final days of Moses (around 1402 BC).

3. Purpose, Themes & Structure

A. The purpose of Exodus is to connect and continue God's covenant with Abraham *(Gen. 12:2)*, through a new covenant with Moses *(Exo. 19:5)*.
   - If Israel kept the covenant with Moses, God promised to make them a "holy nation" *(19:6)*.

B. The theme for Exodus is Israel's change from a captive people under Egypt into a covenant nation under God.

C. The structure of Exodus is in two parts.
   - God delivering His people from slavery in Egypt *(chapters 1-18)*.
   - God's covenant with Israel at Mt. Sinai *(chapters 19-40)*.

4. Historical Background

Exodus tells about the final years (of the 430 years), that Israel spent in Egypt (about 1876-1446 BC). It also records the covenant laws given to Israel through Moses at Mt. Sinai (about 1445 BC).
- Exodus records about the first 80 years of Moses' life.
  ▶ Moses' rescue, adoption and early years *(2:1-14)*.
  ▶ Moses' second forty years *(2:15-25)*.
- Exodus also tells about the ten great plagues that God used to strike Egypt and convince the Pharaoh to let Israel go *(5:1-11:10)*. Refer the following chart:

The Ten Plagues on Egypt

The Plague	Location
Blood	*7:22*
Frogs	*8:6*
Lice	*8:17*
Flies	*8:24*
Diseased livestock	*9:6*
Boils	*9:10*
Hail	*9:23*
Locusts	*10:13*
Darkness	*10:22*
Death of firstborn	*12:29*

5. Development of Message

The message of Exodus can be developed from <u>slavery</u> to <u>redemption</u> to <u>revelation</u> to <u>response</u>.
- Slavery under Egypt *(1:1-4:31)*.
  - ▶ Genesis ended with Israel as Egypt's guests. Exodus begins with Israel as Egypt's slaves. Three hundred and fifty years had passed since the time of Joseph. The Pharaoh of Egypt no longer knew or cared about Joseph *(1:8-14)*. The important thing was the labor provided by the Israelites for Egypt's building projects.
    - ▷ Over time, there were so many Israelites in Egypt that the Pharaoh ordered the Hebrew males killed at birth to control Israel's population *(1:15-22)*.
      - • Moses was born at this time. His sister Miriam saved him from being killed by putting him into a basket in the Nile River. Pharaoh's daughter rescued him from the water and adopted him (2:1-10).
    - ▷ When Moses was an adult, he saw an Egyptian guard beating a Hebrew slave. Moses was so angry that he killed the guard *(2:11-15)*. Pharaoh wanted Moses dead for this act.
    - ▷ Moses ran away to Midian, where he met and married his wife Zipporah. He spent 40 years as a shepherd for her family. Then God spoke to Moses from a burning bush, asking him to lead Israel out of Egypt *(2:16-4:17)*. Moses obeyed God and returned to Egypt *(4:18-31)*.
- Redemption from Egypt *(5:1-19:1)*.
  - ▶ Moses went to the court of Pharaoh to deliver God's command to let Israel go. Pharaoh refused to listen, and made the Israelites do more slave work than they had before (5:1-7:13).
  - ▶ God then sent ten plagues on Egypt to convince Pharaoh to let Israel go *(7:14-12:30.* See the chart "The Ten Plagues on Egypt" above.*)*.
  - ▶ After the tenth plague (death of the firstborn), Pharaoh let Israel go. Israel began its wilderness journey to Mt. Sinai *(12:31-13:22)*. As they traveled, Pharaoh changed his mind and sent the Egyptian army to capture Israel. God led Moses to lead the people to the Red Sea. There, God miraculously parted the waters so all Israel walked across

> **NOTES**

on dry land. God then caused the waters to close on the Egyptian army and destroy them *(14:1-15:27)*.
▶ God then provided food, water, and military success so Israel could safely complete the journey from the Red Sea to Mt. Sinai *(15:22-18:27)*.
- Revelation of the Covenant *(19:1-31:18)*.
▶ God revealed much about His character at Mt. Sinai as He revealed the laws He wanted Israel to keep. The Covenant of Moses (also called the "Mosaic Covenant"), applied to every area of life for God's people.
▷ The commandments *(20:1-26)*, were given to tell the people what God expected of them in their personal lives as they lived before God.
▷ The social laws *(21:1-24:11)*, were given to explain what God expected as they lived amongst each other.
▷ The religious laws *(24:12-31:18)*, were given to explain how they could properly approach God on His terms.
- These laws include instructions on building the tabernacle. The tabernacle was Israel's house of worship that traveled with the Jews from Mt. Sinai through the rest of their wilderness journey.
- Response to the Covenant *(32:1-40:38)*.
▶ Israel's first response to the covenant was to break it by worshiping a golden calf *(32:1-6)*. Moses pleaded with God to keep Israel as His people *(32:7-33:23)*.
▷ God renewed His covenant with Israel *(34:1-35)*.
▷ This time, Israel chose to obey the covenant *(35:1-40:33)*.
▷ God then filled the tabernacle with His glory *(40:34-38)*.

6. Theology

A. God is Savior and Provider *(chapters 1-18)*.
- God saves the infant Moses *(2:1-10)*.
- God saves His people from slavery *(12:21-36)*.
- God saves Israel from the Egyptian army *(14:1-15:27)*.
- God provides the bread of life *(16:1-36*; see *Joh. 6:22-59)*.
- God provides the water of life *(17:1-7*; see *Joh. 4:1-26)*.

B. God is the Holy Lawgiver *(chapters 19-40)*.
- God gives the Ten Commandments to give Israel basic principles how to live a life pleasing to Him *(20:1-26)*.
- God gives instructions on living a holy life toward other people in the Covenant *(21:1-23:33)*.
- God gives instructions on holy living through worship and fellowship with Him *(24:1-31:18)*.
▶ The tabernacle *(chapters 26, 35)* was a traveling tent or sanctuary that Israel used as its place for worship. It was built as God instructed Moses to build it on Mt. Sinai.
▷ The people of Israel supplied the material and labor for building the tabernacle.

> NOTES

▷ God blessed the completed tabernacle by filling its sanctuary with His glory.
▷ The tabernacle was also called "The Tent of Meeting" because it was the main place where God and His people met.
- God gives instructions to restore fellowship with Him through sacrifice *(34:1-40:38)*.

7. Uniqueness and How to Preach It in Your Church Plant

A. Moses is a unique person in the Bible. Time and again, by faith he chooses God's way over what seemed to be easier or more comfortable.
- Choosing Israel over Egypt *(4:18-22*; see *Heb. 11:24-27)*.
- Choosing to lead Israel in keeping the first Passover before the firstborn males were struck down *(12:1-13:22*; see *Heb. 11:28)*.
- Choosing by faith to pass through the Red Sea at God's instruction to escape the Egyptian army *(14:1-15:27*; see *Heb. 11:29)*.

B. God's basic rules for living are The Ten Commandments. Many pastors preach them one at a time. Sometimes, pastors divide the Ten Commandments into two groups.
- Group One: Commandments Relating to God *(20:1-11)*.
  ▶ Only trust God.
  ▶ Only worship God.
  ▶ Use God's name only to honor Him.
  ▶ Use the Sabbath to rest and honor God.
- Group Two: Commandments Relating to People *(20:12-17)*.
  ▶ Honor your parents.
  ▶ Do not murder.
  ▶ Be faithful to your husband or wife.
  ▶ Do not steal.
  ▶ Do not lie.
  ▶ Be content with what God has given you.
- As you preach, help people understand the Law's purposes.
  ▶ The Law is given to guide us through life.
  ▶ The Law reveals God's holiness.
  ▶ The Law reveals man's sin.
  ▶ The Law tells us how to best relate to both God and other people

Assignment:

Find three examples where the Law *(20:1-31:18)* reveals God's holiness. In the spaces provided, write down the examples and the places in the Bible where you found them.

1)

2)

3)

> **NOTES**
>
> Find three examples where the Law reveals man's sin. In the spaces below, write down the examples and the places in the Bible where you found them.
>
> 1)
>
> 2)
>
> 3)

8. Outline of Exodus

A. Israel's Slavery and Release *(chapters 1-18)*.
   - Moses is Prepared *(1:1-4:31)*.
     ▶ Background of Egypt's tyranny *(1:1-22)*.
     ▶ Moses' adoption and first 40 years *(2:1-14)*.
     ▶ Moses' second 40 years *(2:15-25)*.
     ▶ God calls Moses at Mt. Horeb *(3:1-4:31)*.
   - God delivers His people from Egypt *(5:1-18:27)*.
     ▶ God's victory over Egypt through the ten plagues *(5:1-11:10)*.
     ▶ The Passover *(12:1-13:22)*.
     ▶ Crossing of the Red Sea *(14:1-15:27)*.
     ▶ Provision of manna from heaven *(16:1-36)*.
     ▶ Provision of water from the cleft rock *(17:1-7)*.
     ▶ Victory at Rephidim *(17:8-16)*.
     ▶ Organizing Israel *(18:1-27)*.

B. God's Covenant with Israel *(chapters 19-40)*.
   - Seal of holiness *(19:1-31:18)*.
     ▶ Covenant promise *(19:1-25)*.
     ▶ The Ten Commandments *(20:1-26)*.
     ▶ Holy living toward others in the Covenant *(21:1-23:33)*.
     ▶ Holy living and fellowship with God *(24:1-31:18)*.
   - Israel's rebellion and repentance *(32:1-33:23)*.
     ▶ Rebellion and broken fellowship with God *(32:1-35)*.
     ▶ Repentance and intercession by Moses *(33:1-23)*.
   - God's response of continuing forgiveness through sacrifice *(34:1-40:38)*.
     ▶ God renews the covenant *(34:1-35)*.
     ▶ Israel obeys the covenant *(35:1-40:33)*.
     ▶ God fills the tabernacle *(40:34-38)*.

Chapter 3
Leviticus

1. Introduction and Title

A. In Leviticus, God shows His desire to have fellowship with Israel. Leviticus provides and explains the laws God's people needed to follow to live in fellowship with God.
- The last chapters of Exodus tell about the building of the tabernacle (see *Exo. 25-40*). Leviticus begins with descriptions of the sacrifices to be performed in the tabernacle *(Lev. 1-7)*. Leviticus explains how important these sacrifices are to keep one's relationship with God.

B. "Leviticus" is the title given this book in an early Latin version of the Bible. It means "having to do with the Levites (priests)."

2. Authorship and Date

A. Moses is the author of Leviticus.
- Leviticus itself says 56 times that God gave these laws to Moses *(1:1; 4:1; 6:24; 8:1*, are a few examples).

B. Moses may have written much of Leviticus while the Israelites were at Mt. Sinai. Leviticus, along with the rest of the books of the Law, was probably put into a final form sometime around 1402 BC.

3. Purpose, Themes & Structure

A. The purpose of Leviticus was to show the Israelites how they could both worship and walk before God in purity.

B. The theme of Leviticus is holiness, or separation from impurity for the purpose of being used by God (see *19:2*).
- Leviticus teaches about holiness in worship and holiness in everyday life.

C. The structure of Leviticus follows the two kinds of holiness taught in the book.
- Holiness in worship *(chapters 1-17)*.
  ▶ This section teaches about restoring fellowship with God as one comes to worship.
  ▶ It also instructs how to express gratitude to God through giving offerings.
  ▶ It explains the laws the priests must follow to lead Israel in worship.
  ▶ It tells about how to stay ritually clean so one can join in worship at the tabernacle.
  ▶ It explains how to become ritually clean again after one has become unclean.
  ▶ It describes the Day of Atonement.
  ▶ It also tells the right way to offer a blood sacrifice, and instructs Israel not to eat the blood of an animal.

- Holiness in everyday life *(chapters 18-27)*.
  - This section tells how to stay pure sexually.
  - It also describes several other practical laws God wanted Israel to follow, including laws about farming, business, and caring for the poor.
  - It reminds Israel to keep God's commandments with others.
  - It describes the punishments for violating God's laws.
  - It commands purity in the lives of the priests of Israel.
  - It describes the serious penalties for wickedness against God.
  - It tells about seven feasts God commanded that Israel keep.
  - It promised blessings for obeying God, and curses for disobeying Him.

4. Historical Background

Leviticus tells about the month between the building of the wilderness tabernacle *(Exo. 40:17)*, and when Israel left Sinai *(Num. 10:11)*.

5. Development of Message

The message of Leviticus develops through its two major sections.
- First, Israel as a group is told how to stay in a right relationship with God as they approach God through worship *(chapters 1-17)*. These instructions included:
  - How to approach God while in fellowship *(1:1-3:17)*.
  - How to approach God when not in fellowship with Him *(4:1-6; 6:7)*.
  - Laws about purity *(11:1-15:33)*.
  - Laws about National Atonement *(16:1-17:16)*.
- Second, the individuals who make up Israel are instructed to honor and obey God in their everyday lives *(chapters 18-27)*. These instructions included:
  - Rules on sexual behavior between people *(18:1-30)*.
  - Rules on social behavior *(19:1-37)*.
  - How to be set apart (holy), before God *(21:1-27:34)*.

6. Theology

The theology of Leviticus focuses on the holiness of God. The ideas of purity and cleanness all point to the truth that God is Holy *(11:44-45; 18:2-4; 19:3-4, 10; 1 Pet. 1:13-16)*.
- Sacrifices could restore broken fellowship with God.
  - Under the Law sacrifice was the only way to restore and remain in fellowship with God *(1:4; 17:11)*.
  - God granted real forgiveness in response to a right sacrifice *(4:20; 5:10; 6:7)*.
- A right sacrifice included real faith and obedience *(26:31,* see *Psa. 51:16-17)*.
- The sacrifices of Leviticus were good for restoring the covenant between God and His people, but not as complete as the once-for-all sacrifice of Jesus on the cross *(Heb. 10:4; 1 Pet. 3:18)*.

7. Uniqueness and How to Preach It in Your Church Plant

Leviticus shows how important it is to keep your relationship right with God. This is so important to God that He set up a complete system of sacrifices for that purpose. These would need to be followed until the time was right for the once-for-all sacrifice of Jesus on the cross.

- The five offerings in *Leviticus 1:1-6:7* all point to Jesus Christ.[9] See the chart below:

Five Levitical Offerings that Point to Jesus Christ

The Levitical Offering	*How It Points to Christ*
Burnt offering *(Lev. 1:1-17)*	Shows Christ's total submission to His Father's will *(Luk. 22:41-44)*
Grain offering *(Lev. 2:1-16)*	Shows Christ's sinless service *(Heb. 4:14-15)*
Peace offering *(Lev. 3:1-17)*	Illustrates the fellowship between believers and God through the Cross *(Rom. 5:8-11)*
Sin offering *(Lev. 4:1-5:13)*	Pictures Jesus as our sin-bearer *(Heb. 9:27-28)*
Trespass offering *(Lev. 5:14-6:7)*	Illustrates Christ's payment for the harm our sin has caused *(Rom. 5:15-16, 6:23)*

Assignment:

Look again at the five Levitical offerings in the table above. Which of the five offerings do you think best illustrates Jesus Christ's ministry, and why? In the space below, write your answers and support them with Scripture.

NOTES

8. Outline of Leviticus

A. Approaching God through Sacrifice *(1:1-17:16)*.
- Laws of sacrifices and offerings *(1:1-7:38)*.
- Consecration of priests *(8:1-10:20)*.
    ▶ Aaron and his sons consecrated *(8:1-36)*.
    ▶ First sacrifices of new priests *(9:1-24)*.
    ▶ Disobedience of Nadab and Abihu *(10:1-20)*.
- Laws to keep pure *(11:1-15:33)*.
    ▶ About foods *(11:1-47)*.
    ▶ About childbirth *(12:1-8)*.
    ▶ About leprosy *(13:1-14:57)*.
    ▶ About bodily discharges *(15:1-33)*.
- Laws about National Atonement *(16:1-17:16)*.
    ▶ About the Day of Atonement *(16:1-34)*.
    ▶ About the place of sacrifice *(17:1-9)*.
    ▶ About the sanctity of blood *(17:10-16)*.

B. Laws to Continue Fellowship with God *(18:1-27:34)*.
- Practical Holiness *(18:1-20:27)*.
    ▶ About sexual sin *(18:1-30)*.
    ▶ About social order *(19:1-37)*.

Chapter 4
Numbers

1. Introduction and Title

A. Numbers tells about Israel's wilderness wanderings. It describes a major transition in the history of God's people. Numbers records the death of the first wilderness generation *(chapters 1-25)*, and its replacement by the second wilderness generation *(chapters 26-36)*.

B. Like Exodus and Leviticus, Numbers begins with the word "and." This shows that the first four books of the Bible are connected.

C. The book of Numbers has many statistics. It contains population counts, a census of the priests and Levites, and other numerical data. Numbers gets its English name from the Greek translation of the Bible called the Septuagint, which gave the book the title *Arithmoi* – "Numbers" – because of all the numbers in the book.

2. Authorship and Date

A. Moses is the author of Numbers.
- In the Bible, Moses is said to be the author of all five books of the Law. *Numbers 33:2* tells about the detailed records Moses kept about the events he saw.

B. Numbers, along with the rest of the books of the Law, was completed sometime around 1402 BC.

3. Purpose, Themes & Structure

A. The purpose of Numbers was to describe the change from Israel's old generation that left Egypt and sinned in the desert to the new generation that stands on the edge of the Promised Land.
- Numbers also recorded the successes and failures of Israel according to their obedience as they went through the wilderness journey *(see 21:1—25:18)*.

B. The overall theme of Numbers is that God's people can go forward only as far as they trust God.

C. Numbers is structured around two census events.
- The first census begins the story of the first generation of Israelites who would travel through the wilderness *(1:1-25:18)*.
  ▶ This generation did not have enough faith to enter the Promised Land as God told them *(14:1-10)*.
- The second census begins the story of the second generation of Israelites who traveled through the wilderness. They would inherit the Promised Land *(26:1-36:13)*.

4. Historical Background

A. Numbers begins just 13 months after Israel's exodus from Egypt (about 1441 BC), and ends almost 39 years later (about 1402 BC).

B. Numbers tells about Israel's journey from Mt. Sinai through the wilderness to the plains of Moab, just outside the Promised Land.

5. Development of Message

A. The message of Numbers is developed through the story of two generations in Israel. It shows how God's preparation and order bring stability and blessing, and how disobedience and rebellion cause disaster that can bring destruction.

B. The first generation of Israelites was prepared to travel across the Sinai wilderness and enter the Promised Land *(1:1-10:10)*. Yet, their disobedience and rebellion against God brought about forty years of wandering until a new generation was ready to take their place *(14:34)*. This was a time of great disorder and instability in Israel. Only when this new generation was put under God's order, was Israel stable enough to take the Promised Land *(26:1-36:13)*.

6. Theology

A. While the book of Leviticus told more about what the priests and Levites had to do to respect God's holiness, the book of Numbers tells about what God expects from the additional people of Israel. Numbers shows that God is angry with anyone who approaches Him with rebellion or immorality *(13:1-14:45)*. Yet, it also shows that God provides a way to approach and have peace with Him; through priests and sacrifices *(5:1-31; 15:22-29)*. The sacrificial system of Numbers is like the sacrifice of Jesus Christ. However, the sacrifices in Numbers were good only for a season, while the sacrifice of Christ is good forever *(Heb. 9:24-28)*.

B. Numbers also demonstrates how God provides for His people's needs. (This is called God's providence.)
- God provides guidance *(9:15-23)*, and protection *(21:21-35)*.
- God instructed His people in His law *(5, 6, 15, 18, 19, 28, 29, 30)*.
- God provided and protected effective leaders for His people *(16, 17, 27:12-23)*.

7. Uniqueness and How to Preach It in Your Church Plant

The book of Numbers says that God is holy, and shows that it is very important to approach God in the right way. Numbers offers a great opportunity to preach that God is still holy. Numbers also opens the door to share that Jesus Christ has fully met the sacrificial requirements to gain our forgiveness *(see Heb. 9:1-10:18)*. Through Christ, we can approach God and have peace with Him.

Assignment:

From the book of Numbers, tell about two differences between Israel's second wilderness generation and the first. What allowed the second generation to enter the Promised Land? Support your answers with Scripture.

8. Outline of the book of Numbers

A. Israel's First Wilderness Generation is Prepared for the Promised Land *(1:1-10:10)*.
- The People and Priests Are Organized *(1:1-4:49)*.
- Israel is Set Apart for God *(5:1-10:10)*.

B. The First Generation Fails *(10:11-25:18)*.
- Israel Complains, God Provides *(10:11-12:16)*.
- Israel Refuses to Enter the Promised Land *(13:1-14:45)*.
- Israel Rebels *(15:1-19:22)*.
- Israel Fails to Honor and Obey God *(20:1-25:18)*.

C. Israel's Second Wilderness Generation is Prepared for the Promised Land *(26:1-36:15)*.
- Israel Is Reorganized *(26:1-27:23)*.
- Offerings and Vows *(28:1-30:16)*.
- Instructions for Conquering and Settling the Promised Land *(31:1-36:15)*.
- Priestly holiness and duties *(21:1-22:33)*.
- Holy assemblies, consecration symbols, desecration penalties *(23:1-24:23)*.
- Years of Sabbath and Jubilee *(25:1-55)*.
- Blessings for obedience and curses for disobedience *(26:1-46)*.
- Vows and tithes *(27:1-34)*.

Chapter 5
Deuteronomy

1. Introduction and Title

A. Deuteronomy records the last messages from Moses to the generation of Israelites who were about to cross into the Promised Land. Moses encouraged this new generation not to disobey God as had the generation that had left Egypt 40 years before. Deuteronomy tells of the renewed covenant between God and His people, and of Moses' death.

B. The name "Deuteronomy" means "second law." The book does not actually contain a second law. But it does explain God's Law given at Mt. Sinai to a second generation of Israelites.

2. Authorship and Date

A. Moses is the author of Deuteronomy. Deuteronomy affirms this almost 40 times.
- Deuteronomy also records Moses' death. Most scholars believe that someone close to Moses, possibly Joshua, wrote what we know as *Chapter 34* of this book and that Moses wrote the other 33 chapters.

B. Deuteronomy, along with the rest of the books of the Law, was written sometime around 1402 BC.

3. Purpose, Themes & Structure

A. The purpose of Deuteronomy was to encourage God's people to make a fresh commitment to the Lord. Moses wanted Israel to renew the covenant God had established with them at Mt. Sinai.

B. The themes of Deuteronomy are expressed in the three messages Moses gave in the book.
- What God had done for Israel since they left Egypt *(1:1-4:43)*.
- What the covenant required of Israel as they entered the Promised Land *(4:44-26:19)*.
- Moses' encouragement to obey God and predictions about blessings and curses for Israel *(27:1-31:30)*.

C. The structure of Deuteronomy follows that of a treaty between a lord or king and his people. This treaty structure was common in Moses' time. It has six parts.[10]
- An introduction or "preamble" *(seen in 1:1-5)*.
- A history of the relationship between the parties of the treaty *(seen in 1:5-4:43)*.
- A general call of faithfulness to the king *(seen in 4:44-11:32)*.

- Specific actions that will prove the people's faithfulness to the king *(seen in 12-26)*.
- Blessings and curses for obedience or disobedience to the treaty *(seen in 27-30)*.
- Witnesses *(seen in 32:1)*.

4. Historical Background

The events of Deuteronomy happen at the end of Israel's 40-year journey in the wilderness. These events happen between Egypt and Canaan (the Promised Land), around 1405 to 1400 BC. Deuteronomy covers about one month as Israel camps in the plains of Moab and prepares to enter the Promised Land *(2:1-3:29)*.

5. Development of Message

Although Deuteronomy's structure follows that of a treaty, its message is developed through the sermons Moses delivers. The purpose of these messages is to encourage Israel to renew the covenant they made with God at Mt. Sinai.
- Moses begins with a history of God's faithfulness to Israel *(1:5-4:43)*.
- Moses then tells about what Israel must do to show their commitment to their covenant with God *(4:44-26:19)*.
- Moses tells Israel to renew their covenant with God, promising blessings for obedience to God and curses for disobedience *(27:1-30:20)*.

6. Theology

A. Although the structure of Deuteronomy may seem like a typical agreement between a lord and his people, God's love for His people makes His covenant with Israel truly unique.

B. The book of Deuteronomy teaches that love, not legalism, is the basis of the covenant between God and His people.[11] Love is the reason behind God's promises *(4:37; 7:6-8; 33:3)*. The people of the covenant are to obey God because they love Him *(6:5; 10:12, 15; 13:3; 30:16, 20)*.

7. Uniqueness and How to Preach It in Your Church Plant

The book of Deuteronomy strongly emphasizes the covenant between God and His people.
- Since it tells what God has done to show His faithfulness to the covenant *(1:1-4:43)*, you can use Deuteronomy to proclaim God's faithfulness.
- Since it tells how God expects Israel to show their faithfulness to the covenant *(4:44-26:19)*, you can use Deuteronomy to encourage loving and faithful obedience to God.
- Since it tells what God will do in cases of obedience and disobedience to the covenant *(27:1-30:20)*, you can preach from Deuteronomy to help others see the consequences of obedience and disobedience.

> **NOTES**

Assignment:

Find three passages in Deuteronomy where God says He loves His people. What is promised in each passage (blessings, protection, long life, etc.) as a result of God's love? Write both the passage reference and the promise in the spaces below.

1)

2)

3)

8. Outline of the Book of Deuteronomy

   A. What God Has Done for Israel *(1:1-4:43)*.

   B. How Israel Should Live *(4:44-26:19)*.
   - The Ten Commandments and the Love of God *(4:44-11:32)*.
   - Laws of Worship and a Holy Life *(12:1-16:22)*.
   - Civil and Social Life *(17:1-26:19)*.

   C. The Covenant Renewed *(27:1-30:20)*.
   - Honoring the Law *(27:1-26)*.
   - Blessings and Punishments *(28:1-68)*.
   - Review of the Covenant *(29:1-29)*.
   - The Life or Death Choice *(30:1-20)*.

   D. The Leadership Change from Moses to Joshua *(31:1-34:12)*.

Chapter 6
Joshua

1. Introduction and Title

A. Joshua is the first of the twelve historical books in the Old Testament. These twelve books cover about 700 years of history beginning with the entry of Israel into the Promised Land and ending with the return of the Jewish nation from Babylon. Joshua is the story of God's people as they both capture and settle the Promised Land.
   - The historical books cover three periods in Israel's history.
     - ▶ Joshua, Judges and Ruth tell about the time leading up to Israel's kings (about 1405-1070 BC).
       - ▷ *Joshua* tells about Israel taking the Promised Land.
       - ▷ *Judges* tells about the military leaders called "judges" that God used to rescue Israel.
       - ▷ *Ruth* is a love story from the time of Judges that tells of God's loving care.
     - ▶ The books of Samuel, Kings, and Chronicles cover the time of Israel's kings (about 1070-586 BC).
       - ▷ The books of *Samuel* record Israel's early kings Saul and David.
       - ▷ The books of *Kings* tell about the division of Israel into two kingdoms, and the kings who ruled them from Solomon to Zedekiah.
       - ▷ The books of *Chronicles* are histories that emphasize faith in the kings and leaders of Israel. These books cover the same time period as 2 Samuel and the books of Kings.
     - ▶ Ezra, Nehemiah, and Esther record events about God's people after the exile in Babylon (about 537-430 BC).
       - ▷ *Ezra* describes the return of the Jewish people from Babylon to Jerusalem.
       - ▷ *Nehemiah* tells about the rebuilding of Jerusalem's walls after the exiles return from Babylon.
       - ▷ *Esther* tells about God's protection of His people in Persia.

B. Joshua is named for the man Joshua, whose name means: "The Lord Saves." There are many times in Joshua where God works miracles to help Israel defeat its enemies.

2. Authorship and Date

A. Joshua was written almost entirely by Joshua, with minor additions by Eleazar, the high priest and his son Phineas.[12]

B. Eyewitness material makes up a good part of Joshua. That means it was probably completed shortly after the events in the book, possibly around 1350 BC.

3. Purpose, Themes & Structure

A. Joshua's purpose was to show how God fulfilled His promise to give Israel the land of Canaan (the Promised Land). *(See 1:2-6; 21:43).*

B. There are two important themes in Joshua: the possession of the land and the covenant between God and His people.
- God had promised the land to Abraham *(Gen. 12:2-3)*, and to Isaac and his descendants *(Gen. 17:19-21)*.
  ▶ Israel's possessing the land was based on its obedience to God's Law *(10:40; 11:20; 23:9-13)*.
- It was crucial that Israel was faithful to their covenant with God *(1:7-8; 22:5; 24:15)*.
  ▶ Israel renewed the covenant through two ceremonies recorded in Joshua.
    ▷ At Mt. Ebal, Joshua built an altar to the Lord, offered sacrifices, and copied and read the Law of Moses (8:30-35).
    ▷ At Shechem, Joshua wrote down the renewed covenant in the "Book of the Law of God," and set up a large stone as a memorial and witness to the covenant (24:25-27).

C. Joshua is structured in three major parts: the preparation of Israel to enter the Promised Land *(chapters 1-5)*, Israel's taking of Canaan *(chapters 6-13)*, and Israel's settlement of Canaan *(chapters 14-24)*.

4. Historical Background

Most of the events in Joshua probably took place within ten years of the time Israel crossed the Jordan River into the Promised Land (around 1406 BC). The date is determined from Caleb's statement *(see Jos. 14:7-10)*, that it had been 45 years since he had spied out the land *(see Num. 13)*. Israel had spent 38 years wandering in the wilderness *(see Deu. 2:14)*. The seven-year difference is the time between Israel's crossing the Jordan and Caleb's speech.

5. Development of Message

The message of Joshua follows three stages.
- Israel is prepared to enter Canaan *(chapters 1-5)*. This stage of military and spiritual preparation set the stage for Israel's success in Canaan.
- Israel conquers Canaan *(chapters 6-13)*. This stage shows the results of both Israel's obedience and disobedience to God. Since Joshua was quick to obey God and to lead Israel to do the same, Israel was successful in conquering Canaan.
- Israel settles Canaan and enters into God's rest *(chapters 14-24)*. The promise at the beginning of Joshua *(1:13, 15)*, comes to pass as Israel settles Canaan, the Promised Land. Obedience to God leads to a place with Him *(see Heb. 3:4)*.

6. Theology

Joshua shows that God is faithful to and responsible for the success of His people.
- Several times, Joshua says that God was involved in Israel's victories *(chapters 6, 10, 11)*.
- Joshua says that God Himself was the Commander of the Army who brought Israel victory *(5:15)*.
- Joshua also shows that God was faithful to His promises to give Canaan to Abraham and his descendants *(Gen. 12:7; 26:3-4; 28:4)*.

7. Uniqueness and How to Preach It in Your Church Plant

Joshua is very clear in giving God credit for what He did on behalf of Israel as they entered, conquered and settled the Promised Land. For example, God delivered the Amorites to be defeated by Israel *(10:8)*. God caused the sun to stand still to help Israel in battle *(10:12, 13)*. Joshua says that the Lord fought for Israel *(10:14)*. Use this truth to preach that God is the great Defender and Protector of those who love and obey Him.

Assignment:

Find three examples of how Israel obeyed God in Joshua. Write the examples below, and where they are found in the Bible.

1)

2)

3)

Which example above makes you most want to be obedient to God today? Why?

8. Outline of Joshua

A. Israel Prepares to Take the Promised Land *(1:1-5:15)*.
- Joshua, the New Leader *(1:1-18)*.
- Military Preparation *(2:1-5:1)*.
- Spiritual Preparation *(5:2-12)*.
- The Commander of the Lord *(5:13-15)*.

B. Israel Divides and Conquers Canaan *(6:1-13:7)*.
- Central Canaan *(6:1-8:35)*.
- Southern Canaan *(9:1-10:43)*.
- Northern Canaan *(11:1-15)*.
- Summary of the Conquest *(11:16-12:24)*.
- Parts Left Unconquered *(13:1-7)*.

C. Israel Settles Canaan *(13:8-24:33)*.
- Settlement Boundaries East of the Jordan *(13:8-33)*.
- Settlement Boundaries West of the Jordan *(14:1-19:51)*.
- The Religious Community Settlement *(20:1-21:42)*.
- Conditions to Remain in the Land *(22:1-24:33)*.

Chapter 7
Judges

1. Introduction and Title

A. Judges is another historical book. It tells about God rescuing the nation of Israel through several bold leaders called "judges." These judges often combined the roles of military leader and governor. They were the leaders God used between the time of Joshua and the time of Israel's kings. During the time of Judges, Israel constantly disobeyed God and almost destroyed themselves.

B. The book of Judges is named for the judges God appointed to lead His people. "Judges" is the title of the book not only in the early Greek and Latin translations of the Bible, but also in the Hebrew version of the book itself.

2. Authorship and Date

A. Tradition says that Samuel, perhaps with his school of prophets, compiled Judges.

B. Scholars believe that Judges was completed between the time Saul became king (1051 BC), and David's conquest of Jerusalem (1004 BC).

3. Purpose, Themes & Structure

A. The purpose of Judges was to show the results of disobedience to God, and finally the need for a righteous king who would lead Israel to God.

B. The themes of Judges focus on the ongoing disobedience of Israel as they fail to learn from their mistakes. This is contrasted with the continuing faithfulness of God as He works to rescue His people through the judges.
   - Israel's failure to complete the conquest of Canaan is connected to their lack of faith and lack of obedience *(2:1-3)*.
   - God's faithfulness to the covenant was shown by sparing Israel through the leadership of the judges *(2:16, 18)*.

C. Judges is structured to demonstrate Israel's cycle of decay during this time. It begins by noting Israel's failure to complete the conquest of Canaan *(1:1-2:5)*. It continues with the stories of the judges *(2:6-16:31)*, as they rescue Israel from their downward spiral of disobedience. Judges concludes with a series of stories that demonstrate Israel's extreme immorality and need for God's ultimate rescue *(chapters 17-21)*.

> **NOTES**

4. Historical Background

A. Judges is the historical sequel to the book of Joshua. The books are linked by their accounts of Joshua's death *(see Jos. 24:29-31 and Jud. 2:6-9)*. While the book of Joshua emphasized an Israel that conquered Canaan through trusting God, Judges tells the story of an unfaithful Israel who suffered frequent defeat because they disobeyed God.

B. The period of judges in Israel began with Joshua's death in about 1375 BC and ended about 1050 BC when Saul was made king of Israel.

5. Development of Message

A. Judges develops its message to show the complete spiritual decay of Israel by the end of the book. Early in Judges, God pronounces His judgment upon Israel for their disobedience and lack of faith *(see chapter 2)*. The last verse of Judges *(21:25)* says that everyone in Israel at that time was devoted to their own interests and nothing more.

B. The message in Judges is developed through seven cycles of oppression and deliverance *(chapters 3-16)*. Each cycle had five parts or steps:
   - Israel's sin.
   - Israel is oppressed.
   - Israel cries out to God for help.
   - God saves Israel.
   - Israel enters into a time of rest.
     ▶ One example of this cycle is found in Judges *3:7-11*.
        ▷ Israel's sin: serving idols *(3:7)*.
        ▷ Israel is oppressed by the Arameans *(3:8)*.
        ▷ Israel cries out to God for help *(3:9a)*.
        ▷ God saves Israel through the judge Othniel *(3:9b-10)*.
        ▷ Israel enters into a time of rest: 40 years *(3:11)*.

C. At the end of the seventh such cycle are stories that demonstrate the personal and national corruption in Israel *(chapters 17-21)*.
   - A man named Micah (not the prophet), had idols made for his house. He hired a priest to manage his household place of idolatry. Later the tribe of Dan stole both Micah's idols and his priest so they could have their own tribal religion *(chapters 17-18)*.
   - A group of perverted men from the tribe of Benjamin raped and murdered a Levite's concubine. The crime was so disturbing that the Levite cut the concubine's body into twelve pieces so each tribe in Israel would know about it. Israel fought against Benjamin, nearly killing all the men of that tribe *(chapters 19-20)*.

6. Theology

The theology of Judges emphasizes the importance of God's mercy and grace. Israel constantly fails to obey God *(see 2:2)*. Often, Israel worships other gods *(2:11-19)*. Yet, God is faithful to His promises to Abraham and his descendants *(2:1)*. He delivers Israel through the judges. God proves Himself to be the faithful partner of the covenant, while Israel violates the covenant in almost every way they can.

- This is like God's grace and mercy shown to us through Jesus Christ. While we were sinners, Christ died for us *(Rom. 6:23)*. It is according to His mercy that we are saved *(Tit. 3:5)*. There is no question that God is the One Who delivers us in spite of our sin.

7. Uniqueness and How to Preach It in Your Church Plant

A. We live in a world that often encourages us to do whatever we want to do. Judges shows us that if everyone followed that advice, disaster would come.

B. When Judges ends, it notes with great sadness that everyone in Israel was doing *"what was right in his own eyes" (21:25)*.

C. Judges has many examples to prove how important it is to obey God, and how a nation will crumble into chaos if it does not *(see 2:19)*.

Assignment:

Find three Scripture passages in Judges that remind you of the world today, and tell how they remind you of today's world in the spaces below.

1)

2)

3)

If you could tell the world one thing you learned from Judges, what would it be? Use Scripture to support your answer.

NOTES

8. Outline of Judges

A. Israel's Deterioration *(1:1-3:4)*.
- Israel Fails to Complete its Mission *(1:1-36)*.
- God Judges Israel for Its Failure *(2:1-3:4)*.

B. Israel is Delivered Seven Times through Six Campaigns *(3:5-16:31)*.
- The Southern Campaign: The Judges Othniel, Ehud and Shamgar *(3:5-31)*.
- The Northern Campaign: The Judges Deborah and Barak *(4:1-5:31)*.
- The Central Campaign: The Judges Gideon, Abimelech, Tola and Jair *(6:1-10:5)*.
- The Eastern Campaign: The Judge Jephthah *(10:6-12:7)*.
- The Second Northern Campaign: The Judges Izban, Elon, and Abdon *(12:8-15)*.
- The Western Campaign: The Judge Samson *(13:1-16:31)*.

C. Israel's Evil *(17:1-21:25)*.
- Idolatry *(17:1-18:31)*.
- Immorality *(19:1-30)*.
- War within Israel *(20:1-21:25)*.

Chapter 8
Ruth

1. Introduction and Title

A. Ruth is a story of love and redemption. Ruth is a Moabite woman who, for the sake of love and family, leaves her home and her heritage in exchange for life with the people and God of Israel.

B. The book of Ruth is named for its main character, Ruth.

2. Authorship and Date

A. Although no one knows for sure, tradition holds that Samuel and his school of prophets are responsible for writing Ruth.

B. Ruth was written sometime around David's anointing as king in 1000 BC.

3. Purpose, Themes & Structure

A. The purpose of Ruth is to show God's loving care. His providence and redemption are always active, even though we don't always see Him working.

B. The themes in Ruth are redemption and God's desire for all to believe in Him.
- The redemption theme is illustrated through Boaz, who is the kinsman-redeemer for Naomi and Ruth. A kinsman-redeemer would have the responsibility of paying the price to redeem a poorer relative out of slavery *(see Lev. 25:47-49)*, or to redeem family land that had been sold *(see Rut. 4:4, 6; Lev. 25:25)*. Boaz illustrates how God redeems us through Jesus Christ.
  ▶ The kinsman-redeemer must be related by blood to those he redeems *(see Deu. 25:5, 7-10; Joh. 1:14; Heb. 2:14-15)*.
  ▶ The kinsman-redeemer must pay the redemption price *(see Rut. 2:1; 1 Pet. 1:18, 19)*.
  ▶ The kinsman redeemer must be a willing redeemer *(see Rut. 3:11; Joh. 10:15, 18)*.
- The theme that salvation can extend to all who follow God is clear from the example of Ruth, who begins the story outside of Israel and ends as the great-grandmother of Israel's King David *(see Rut. 4:13-22; Mat. 1:3-6)*.

C. Ruth is structured to highlight Ruth's demonstration of love *(chapters 1, 2)* and God's reward for her love *(chapters 3, 4)*.

NOTES

4. Historical Background

Ruth's story is set in the time of the judges in Israel *(1:1)*, probably around 1100 BC. This was a time of great immorality and faithlessness in Israel. Even as a Moabite woman, Ruth is recognized in this book of the Bible as a woman of virtue in the midst of Israel's decay *(3:11)*.

5. Development of Message

The message develops around Ruth's decisions that demonstrate her integrity and faith.
- Her decision to stay with Naomi *(1:16-18)*.
- Her decision to care for Naomi *(2:11)*.
- Her decision to obey Naomi *(3:6-9)*.
- The result of Ruth's decision: redemption by Boaz, her kinsman-redeemer *(4:1-10)*.

6. Theology

A. Ruth shows God's guidance and hand in the lives of common people. He is in control of every situation, no matter how big or small.
- God draws Naomi back to Bethlehem *(1:6)*.
- God gives Naomi an heir *(4:13)*.
- God answers the prayers of the people in Ruth as they ask for His blessing and leading *(1:8-9; 2:12, 20; 3:10)*.

B. Redemption is an important point of theology in Ruth.
- Boaz offers redemption by providing payment to buy back the land of Naomi *(4:4-9)*. He also redeems the family line by marrying Ruth and having a son with her *(4:13)*.
- Boaz is an example of Jesus' redemption. Jesus offers rescue by making Himself our payment. His sacrifice buys us freedom from the bondage of sin (see *Gal. 1:3-5; Tit. 2:14*).

7. Uniqueness and How to Preach It in Your Church Plant

Ruth's series of decisions to be loyal, obedient and righteous in everyday life helped make history. Her union with Boaz made her the great-grandmother of King David *(4:17-22)*. Obedience to God in our everyday lives may not show many results. However, God can use our everyday decisions to obey Him to make history we may never know about until we are in heaven.

NOTES

Assignment:

Find three verses in Ruth that tell about Ruth's character. List both the verse numbers and what they tell about Ruth's character below.

1)

2)

3)

Find three verses in Ruth that tell about Boaz' character. List both the verse numbers and what they tell about Boaz' character below.

1)

2)

3)

8. Outline of Ruth

    A. From Moab to Bethlehem *(1)*.
- Tragedy in Moab *(1:1-5)*.
- Ruth Decides to Stay with Naomi *(1:6-22)*.

    B. Ruth Cares for Naomi and Meets Boaz *(2)*.

    C. Naomi and Ruth Seek Redemption from Boaz *(3)*.

    D. Boaz Redeems Ruth *(4)*.
- Boaz Marries Ruth *(4:1-12)*.
- Ruth is the Great-Grandmother of David *(4:13-22)*.

Chapter 9
1 Samuel

1. Introduction and Title

A. The historical books 1 and 2 Samuel were originally one book. The ancient Greek Bible called the Septuagint was the first to divide the books. 1 Samuel covers the ninety-four year period from Samuel's birth to Saul's death. This period includes the change in Israel from the time of judges to the time of kings.

B. The books of Samuel are named for the prophet Samuel, who is a main character.

2. Authorship and Date

A. Scholars are not sure who finally put together 1 and 2 Samuel. The book itself says that Samuel wrote down records of Israel *(1 Sam. 10:25)*. *1 Chronicles 29:29* says that prophets like Samuel, Gad, and Nathan recorded many events of King David's life. It is likely that a prophet put together these and other writings to compile the books of Samuel.

B. The books of Samuel were written around 926 B.C.

3. Purpose, Themes & Structure

A. The purpose of 1 Samuel is to show how God's authority over Israel was demonstrated through Israel's kings, and especially through the rise of David.

B. The themes of 1 Samuel include Israel's change in government from judges to kings; and that the consequences of sin affect rulers as much as anyone else *(see 15:23)*.

C. 1 Samuel is structured around the lives of the prophet Samuel *(chapters 1-7)*, Israel's first king, Saul *(chapters 8-31)*, and David, Israel's greatest king who was yet to be enthroned *(chapters 16-31)*.

4. Historical Background

A. 1 Samuel is set in the ninety-four year period between Samuel's birth (around 1105 BC), and Saul's defeat and death at Gilboa (around 1011 BC). During this time, the people of Israel beg for a king like many other nations. Their request for a king is, in a way, a rejection of God's own rule. Yet, God grants their request. Israel changes its government from a loose association of tribes to a strong central king.

B. During the events of 1 Samuel, the Philistines are often (but not always) the enemy met in battle.

5. Development of Message

The message of God's ultimate rule through those He places in authority is developed through the leaders of Israel who come and go in 1 Samuel. God removes his blessing from one to make way for the next because of sin in a leader's life in each of the following cases.
- The transition from Eli to Samuel *(chapters 1-3)*.
- The transition from Samuel to Saul *(chapters 8-12)*.
- The transition from Saul to David *(13:5-18:9)*.

6. Theology

A. 1 Samuel's theology centers on the rule of God over all things. Here, God's rule is established through a strong central kingship that begins with Saul and continues through David.

B. 1 Samuel's theology also shows that no one, not even prophets and kings, can disobey God and expect to achieve what He wants. A clear commitment to God's guidance and direction is expected of leaders. Without it, they will fail.

7. Uniqueness and How to Preach It in Your Church Plant

1 Samuel clearly shows both the strengths and weaknesses of it main characters.
- Samuel was a strong national leader as a judge and prophet, but weak in terms of leading his family into righteousness (see *3:19-21; 8:1-9*). Preach the need for leaders of men to be leaders at home.
- Saul was a strong warrior in battle, but could not win the battle over his own will to obey God's commands (see *13:5-15:9*). Preach the need to win the battle over one's own will through obedience to God.

Assignment:

Based on the wisdom in 1 Samuel, what three points of advice would you offer people who would like to be leaders? Use passages from 1 Samuel to support your points.

1)

2)

3)

8. Outline of 1 Samuel

A. The Last Judge of Israel: Samuel *(1-7)*.
   - The Leadership Change from Eli to Samuel *(1:1-3:21)*.
   - Samuel as Judge of Israel *(4:1-7:17)*.

B. The First King of Israel: Saul *(8-31)*.
   - The Leadership Change from Samuel to Saul *(8:1-12:25)*.
   - Saul as King of Israel *(13:1-15:9)*.
     - ▶ Successes *(13:1-4)*.
     - ▶ Failures *(13:5-15:9)*.
   - The Leadership Change from Saul to David *(15:10-31:13)*.
     - ▶ God Rejects Saul as King *(15:10-15:35)*.
     - ▶ David Anointed as King *(16:1-13)*.
     - ▶ David the Musician *(16:14-23)*.
     - ▶ David and Goliath *(17:1-58)*.
     - ▶ David Flees from Saul *(18:1-30:31)*.
     - ▶ Saul's Last Battle and Death *(31:1-13)*.

Chapter 10
2 Samuel

1. Introduction and Title (see 1 Samuel Title)

2 Samuel tells about David's reign. It records the major events of David's forty-year rule. David reigned first over Judah for seven years, then over Judah and Israel for the next thirty-three years. 2 Samuel also records David's sins of adultery, murder and the effects of those sins on David's family and his kingship.

2. Authorship and Date (see 1 Samuel Authorship/Date)

3. Purpose, Themes & Structure

A. The purpose of 2 Samuel continues from 1 Samuel: to show how God's authority over Israel was demonstrated, particularly, through the rise and rule of King David. The book makes it clear that God was still the true King of Israel.

B. The theme of 2 Samuel is that the key to David's reign, when it was successful, was David's relationship with God. Even as a king, David usually remembered to turn to God for direction and strength *(2:1; 5:19)*.
   - David is also shown as an ideal leader over an imperfect kingdom. David points toward Christ in this way. Christ, too, would be a perfect and ideal leader although His kingdom would be new and without blemish.

C. 2 Samuel is structured around David's triumphs *(chapters 1-10)*, his personal sins *(chapter 11)*, and the troubles that follow for both his family and the nation *(chapters 12-24)*. David's life and career are on the rise until he deliberately commits the sins of adultery and murder. Although David repents, the consequences of those sins cause breakdowns in his family and in Israel.

4. Historical Background

Although Saul was the first king in Israel, David was the king that completed Israel's shift from the time of judges to the time of kings. 2 Kings tells about how Judah and Israel united early in David's forty-year rule (about 1011 to 971 BC). It also tells about the major military, political, and personal events in David's life during those years.

5. Development of Message

The key message of 2 Samuel is that obedience to God brings blessing, while disobedience to God brings trouble. 2 Samuel makes David's life a perfect example of this message.
   - *2 Samuel 1-10* builds on the political, spiritual, and military victories of David.

- In *2 Samuel 11*, David commits the sins of adultery and murder. Even within that chapter, the results of those sins damage both David's family and his integrity as a king.
- *2 Samuel 12-24* records the troubles of David's political and personal life.

6. Theology

God's continuing redemption is evident in 2 Samuel. It is demonstrated not only in the covenant God makes with David *(7:4-17)*, but also through David's personal life.
- God redeems David's desire to build a house for the Lord by announcing His desire to build a house for David *(7:1-2)*.
  ▶ God's house for David is a family line *(7:11-13)*, through which the Messiah would be born (see *Mat. 1:1, 16; Luk. 3:23*).
  ▶ David's line would also have a perpetual kingdom and throne. This is fulfilled immediately through David's family line of kings, and finally through Jesus.
  ▶ This covenant would not be broken, but the kings would be punished for their disobedience *(7:14-15)*.
- God redeems David's personal life through mercy and forgiveness as David turns to God in humility and repentance *(12:13-14;* see *Psa. 51)*.

7. Uniqueness and How to Preach It in Your Church Plant

Through the example of David's life, 2 Samuel shows how God works in a covenant relationship with people who love Him.
- 2 Samuel makes it clear that obedience to God brings blessing, while disobedience brings trouble. <u>This is not to say that obedience always brings about the results we want.</u> However, obedience brings the blessing of a closer relationship with God. Disobedience puts distance in our relationship with God. Being faithful to God can see us through the most difficult situations.
- David's covenant relationship with God is one example of God's grace and mercy staying with a person even though sin may bring trouble *(7:14-15)*.
- David's example demonstrates the power of repentance in restoring our relationship with God *(12:13-14, 24-31)*.
- David's example also demonstrates that there are always consequences to sin *(12:15-23)*.

Assignment:

What encouragement do you take from the example of David's life in 2 Samuel? Use Scripture to support your answers.

What warnings do you take from the example of David's life in 2 Samuel? Use Scripture to support your answers.

8. Outline of 2 Samuel

    A. David's Victories *(1-10)*.
- Political Victories *(1-5)*.
  - David's Sorrow over the Deaths of Saul and Jonathan *(1:1-27)*.
  - David Anointed King over Judah *(2:1-7)*.
  - Battles and Murders in the Struggle for Israel *(2:8-4:12)*.
  - Judah and Israel Unite under David *(5:1-16)*.
  - David Defeats the Philistines *(5:17-25)*.
- Spiritual Victories *(6-7)*.
  - The Ark Returns to the City of David *(6:1-23)*.
  - God's Covenant with David *(7:1-29)*.
- Military Victories *(8-10)*.
  - Victories over Philistia, Moab, Zobah and Syria *(8:1-12)*.
  - David's Righteous Rule *(8:13-9:13)*.
  - Victories over Ammon and Syria *(10:1-19)*.

NOTES

B. David's Sins *(11)*.
- Adultery with Bathsheba *(11:1-5)*.
- Murder of Uriah *(11:6-27)*.
  ▶ David and Bathsheba Marry *(11:26-27)*.

C. David's Troubles *(12-24)*.
- David's Family Troubles *(12:1-13:36)*.
  ▶ Nathan's Prophecy *(12:1-12)*.
  ▶ David Repents *(12:13-14)*.
  ▶ One Son Dies, Another Is Given *(12:15-25)*.
  ▶ Incest in David's Family (13:1-20).
  ▶ Absalom Murders Amnon *(13:21-36)*.
- David's Kingdom Troubles *(13:37-24:25)*.
  ▶ Absalom Rebels against David *(13:37-17:29)*.
  ▶ The Murder of Absalom *(18:1-33)*.
  ▶ David Is Restored to Power *(19:1-20:26)*.
  ▶ Famine and War *(21:1-22)*.
  ▶ David Gives Thanks and a Final Word *(22:1-23:7)*.
  ▶ David's Mighty Men *(23:8-39)*.
  ▶ The Census and the Plague *(24:1-25)*.

Chapter 11
1 Kings

1. Introduction and Title

A. 1 and 2 Kings were originally one book. Together, they offer a political history of Israel from the time of Solomon until the beginning of the Babylonian captivity. 1 Kings tells about the rule of Solomon when Judah and Israel were united, and then about many kings that followed when the kingdoms were divided.

B. The title of 1 and 2 Kings came from the Latin Vulgate. The division of 1 and 2 Kings into two books happened centuries before in the Septuagint. The Septuagint called these books "3 and 4 Kingdoms," having titled 1 and 2 Samuel "1 and 2 Kingdoms."

2. Authorship and Date

A. The identity of the author is unknown. Some scholars have suggested that a Jew in exile in Babylon, such as Ezra or Nehemiah, may have written 1 and 2 Kings. Jewish tradition says the author is Jeremiah.

B. The likely date for the completion of 1 and 2 Kings is between 560 and 538 BC.

3. Purpose, Themes & Structure

A. The purpose of 1 and 2 Kings is to record both the history of the kings of Israel and Judah, and the spiritual lessons learned from their rule.

B. The theme of both 1 and 2 Kings is to measure the kings of Israel and Judah according to their obedience to the Law of Moses, and the covenants of Abraham and David.

C. The first section *(chapters 1-11)*, records Solomon's rule over the united kingdom of Israel. The second section *(chapters 12-22)*, tells about the divided kingdoms of Israel, Judah, and the many kings who ruled them.

4. Historical Background

1 Kings covers about the 120 years from the beginning of Solomon's reign (971 BC), through the end of Ahaziah's reign (851 BC). During this time, the united kingdom of Israel split into the two kingdoms of Israel and Judah (931 BC).

5. Development of Message

The message of 1 Kings is that a divided heart results in a divided kingdom. 1 Kings tells about the good days at the beginning of Solomon's reign *(chapters 1-8)*. Then it records his decline as a king and a man of God *(chapters 9-11)*. Solomon's heart was divided between the God of his father David, and the gods of the many foreign wives he had *(11:1-8)*. As a result of Solomon's disobedience, God caused the kingdom to be divided *(11:9-13)*.

- Prophets are active in 1 Kings. They remind the rulers of Israel and Judah of their responsibilities to obey God *(18:17-18)*. Through their miracles, they help remind the people that God loves them and is ready to help *(17:17-24)*. Elijah is the most visible prophet in 1 Kings *(chapters 17-19)*.

6. Theology

1 Kings shows that God evaluates kings and men by different standards than those of the world system. The kings of the covenant are judged not by how big or wealthy their kingdoms were, but by how obedient they were to God's laws and covenants. King Omri is known by some scholars as the greatest king of Israel because his territory and alliances were so big. However, 1 Kings evaluates Omri by God's standards. He did evil in God's sight, and is only discussed in eight verses *(16:21-28)*. On the other hand, 1 Kings describes David as the standard Solomon should have lived by *(11:4, 6)*.

7. Uniqueness and How to Preach It in Your Church Plant

1 Kings shows the important differences between God's standards and the world system's standards. There are several examples of kings who seemed to be successful in getting what they wanted. Yet, those same kings are often seen as failures in the eyes of God, because they did evil *(16:30)*. They may have thought their disobedience didn't matter, but they were wrong *(Pro. 14:12)*. The standards we use to measure our lives do matter. Encourage people to follow God's greatest standard, Jesus Christ *(1 Cor. 11:1; Phi. 2:5-11)*.

Assignment:

Look at the Bible verses below about two kings. List what each king did. Are the things recorded about them spiritual or political?

Asa *(1 Kings 15:9-15)*

Ahab *(1 Kings 18:29-33)*

8. Outline of 1 Kings

A. The United Kingdom *(1:1-11:43)*.
- Solomon Begins His Reign *(1:1-2:46)*.
- Solomon's Rise *(3:1-8:66)*.
- Solomon's Decline *(9:1-11:43)*.

B. The Divided Kingdom *(12:1-22:53)*.
- The Kingdom Divides under Jeroboam and Rehoboam *(12:1-14:31)*.
- Abijam and Asa of Judah *(15:1-24)*.
- Nadab, Baasha, Elah, Zimri and Omri of Israel *(15:25-16:28)*.
- King Ahab of Israel and the Prophet Elijah *(16:29-22:40)*.
- Jehoshaphat of Judah *(22:41-50)*.
- Ahaziah of Israel *(22:51-53)*.

NOTES

Chapter 12
2 Kings

1. Introduction and Title (see 1 Kings Title)

2 Kings records the history of the divided kingdoms Israel and Judah, as both nations finally reject obedience to their covenant with God and go into exile and captivity.

2. Authorship and Date (see 1 Kings Authorship/Date)

3. Purpose, Themes & Structure

A. The purpose of 1 and 2 Kings is to record both the history of the kings of Israel and Judah, and the spiritual lessons learned from their rule.

B. The common theme of 1 and 2 Kings is to measure the kings of Israel and Judah according to their obedience to the covenants of Abraham, David and the Law of Moses. This standard is applied when the writer says *"a king did evil or right in the eyes of the Lord" (3:2; 18:3)*.

C. 2 Kings is structured around the stories of the kingdoms it tells about. The book begins with the stories of the divided kingdom of Israel and Judah *(chapters 1-18)*. The first section of 2 Kings ends with Israel falling captive to Assyria (722 BC). The second section *(chapters 19-25)*, tells about the kingdom and kings of Judah from the time Israel falls, until Judah is taken into captivity by Babylon (587 BC).

4. Historical Background

2 Kings tells about the final 131 years of the divided kingdoms of Israel and Judah from the reign of King Ahaziah of Israel (starting in 853 BC), until the fall of Israel into Assyrian captivity (722 BC). It then continues to tell about the additional 136 years of the kingdom of Judah before it fell into Babylonian captivity (587 BC).

5. Development of Message

The message of 2 Kings is that kings are just as responsible to live by God's standards as anyone else. As in much of the Old Testament, the success or failure of the kings of Israel and Judah is measured by their obedience to God's covenants and laws. The ultimate failure of these kings to obey God brought about God's judgment of foreign captivity to Israel *(17:7-23)*, and Judah *(23:31-25:21)*.
- Just as Elijah was the most visible prophet in 1 Kings, Elisha is the most visible prophet in 2 Kings. 2 Kings records many miracles of Elisha as he ministers to both kings and common people *(chapters 3-8)*.

6. Theology

2 Kings shows that God controls both history and human activity. It tells again that obedience to God brings favor, and disobedience brings trouble. It also shows God's determination to redeem His people and stay faithful to His promises, even when His people are disobedient. In the midst of great evil, God preserved David's family line of the covenant *(11:1-3)*. The release of King Jehoiachin in Babylon at the end of the book is another sign that God is not finished with His covenant people *(25:27-30; Jer. 52:31-34)*.

7. Uniqueness and How to Preach It in Your Church Plant

2 Kings often tells about people who are in great trouble. It can be a king who needs military help *(6:8-18)*, or a widow who needs a way out of debt *(4:1-7)*. 2 Kings shows that God is always ready to help people who turn to Him. He is faithful when we are not. When people want to change their lives to please God, they sometimes wonder if God will help them make those changes. Preach that God is ready to help *(Psa. 46:1; Heb. 4:14-16)* and will bring forth change.

Assignment:

Read *2 Kings 4-8*. Find three examples of God helping someone in trouble and list them below.

1)

2)

3)

8. Outline of 2 Kings

    A. The Divided Kingdom *(1:1-17:41)*.
- Two Kings of Israel and Elisha the Prophet *(1:1-8:15)*.
- Two Kings of Judah *(8:16-9:29)*.
- Jehu of Israel *(9:30-10:26)*.
- Queen Athaliah of Judah *(11:1-16)*.
- Covenant Renewed: Joash of Judah *(11:17-12:21)*.
- More Kings of Israel and Elisha the Prophet *(13:1-25)*.
- Amaziah of Judah *(14:1-22)*.
- Jeroboam II of Israel *(14:23-29)*.
- Azariah of Judah *(15:1-7)*.
- Five Kings of Israel *(15:8-31)*.
- Two Kings of Judah *(15:32-16:20)*.
- Hoshea of Israel and the Assyrian Captivity *(17:1-41)*.

B. The Kingdom of Judah *(18:1-25:30)*.
- Hezekiah, Manasseh and Amon of Judah *(18:1-21:26)*.
- Covenant Renewed: Josiah of Judah *(22:1-23:30)*.
- Jehoahaz and Jehoiakim of Judah *(23:31-24:7)*.
- Jehoiachin of Judah; Babylon Takes Captives *(24:8-16)*.
- Zedekiah of Judah; Babylon Takes Over *(24:17-25:30)*.

Chapter 13
1 Chronicles

1. Introduction and Title

   A. 1 and 2 Chronicles were originally one book. The books were separated in the Greek Old Testament called the Septuagint. The Chronicles cover the same time in Jewish history as 2 Samuel through 2 Kings. Though about one-half of the material is repeated in earlier Old Testament books, there is a difference between Samuel/Kings and Chronicles. Chronicles tells about this history from the viewpoint of those Jews who returned from exile in Persia to rebuild Jerusalem.

   B. The Chronicles take their title from Jerome's *Latin Vulgate*, which titled them *The Chronicles of the Whole of Sacred History*.

2. Authorship and Date

   A. Scholars are not certain who wrote Chronicles. Jewish tradition says the Chronicles are the work of Ezra.

   B. Many scholars place the date of the completion of Chronicles around 425 BC.

3. Purpose, Themes & Structure

   A. The purpose of 1 Chronicles was to inspire the remnant of Israel (who had returned to Jerusalem to rebuild their nation and the temple), to trust God and His promises.

   B. The theme of 1 Chronicles is that God Himself founded David's kingdom because of His covenant promises to Abraham, Isaac and Jacob *(17:12)*.[13] The rebuilding of the temple in Jerusalem also becomes an important theme at the end of 1 Chronicles.

   C. 1 Chronicles is structured in two major sections. The first *(chapters 1-9)*, tells about David's royal family line. Chronicles is one of two books in the Bible to cover all of human history from creation to the author's day. Matthew and Chronicles use genealogies (lists of family generations) to accomplish this. The second section *(chapters 10-29)*, tells about David's reign as king.

4. Historical Background

   1 Chronicles first notes David's family line from the time of Adam. Then it tells about David's reign as king of Israel (1010-971 BC). The book is written from a priestly perspective. 1 Chronicles emphasizes God's covenant with David through major events in David's life.

NOTES

5. Development of Message

1 Chronicles tells about the connection between the Jewish exiles and God's promises. It makes the connection that God's promises were still in effect for the exiles. Its message develops in three stages.
- It begins by showing David's family line and his connection to Judah, through whom the Messiah would come *(2:3-15*; see *Gen. 49:10)*.
- It continues with God's covenant with David *(17:1-27)*.
- It then demonstrates that David's kingdom was established on the true worship of God; just as David and the priests of his time showed *(chapters 13, 15, 16)*.

6. Theology

1 Chronicles shows that God alone deserves our worship and honor (see *16:29; 17:20)*. It also shows that true worship of God connects us with generations of God's people of faith *(17:21-22*; see *Heb. 11)*. God's faithfulness to His promises were true for David and are true for all generations of His people *(16:14-24)*.

7. Uniqueness and How to Preach It in Your Church Plant

Worship means to revere, and give honor to the worth of someone or something. 1 Chronicles shows that David wanted to make the worship of God a central part of life in Israel. 1 Chronicles has more information about David's relationship with God and worship in Israel than it does about David's military victories. To God, <u>worship and a right relationship with Him</u>, are far more important than armies and politics. People today need to hear about the importance of true worship. Preach that God alone deserves worship *(16:25-27; Psa. 29:2)*. Preach to worship God with a heart full of thanks for all He has done *(16:8-13; Psa. 103)*. Remind people that true worship of God also means obedience to Him *(1 Sam. 15:22)*.

Assignment:

1 Chronicles shows that God is faithful to the promises He makes. Read *1 Chronicles 17:7-14*. In the space below list the promises God made to David in this covenant, along with the verse numbers where the promises are found.

8. Outline of 1 Chronicles

A. Family Lines from Adam to David *(1:1-9:44)*.
   - From Adam to Jacob *(1:1-2:2)*.
   - Jacob's Generations *(2:2-9:44)*.

B. History of King David *(10:1-29:30)*.
   - Saul's Death *(10:1-14)*.
   - David and His Heroes *(11:1-12:40)*.
   - Attempt to Move the Ark *(13:1-14)*.
   - David's Rule Established *(14:1-17)*.
   - The Ark Arrives *(15:1-16:43)*.
   - God's Covenant with David *(17:1-27)*.
   - David's Military Victories *(18:1-20:8)*.
   - The Census *(21:1-22:1)*.
   - David's Preparations for Solomon *(22:2-29:30)*.
     - ▶ Temple Preparations *(22:2-19)*.
     - ▶ Religious and Political Preparations *(23:1-27:34)*.
     - ▶ The Great Assembly *(28:1-29:22)*.
     - ▶ Solomon Becomes King *(28:22-30)*.

NOTES

Chapter 14
2 Chronicles

1. **Introduction and Title (see 1 Chronicles Introduction/Title)**

2. **Authorship and Date (see 1 Chronicles Authorship/Date)**

3. **Purpose, Themes & Structure**

    A. The purpose of 2 Chronicles was to remind the remnant of Israel that even though the kings after David were not always faithful, God was still faithful to His covenant promises to David.

    B. The theme of 2 Chronicles is God's commitment to His covenant with David in the time of the kings after David's death.[14] The dedication, decline, and destruction of the temple are also major themes in this book.

    C. 2 Chronicles is structured in two major sections. The first *(chapters 1-9)*, tells about Solomon's reign as king. The second *(chapters 10-36)*, tells about the many kings of the divided kingdoms of Israel and Judah. This covers until Cyrus decreed that the Jewish exiles in Persia could return and rebuild Jerusalem (538 BC).

4. **Historical Background**

    2 Chronicles tells about the time between the start of Solomon's reign (971 BC); through the time of Cyrus' edict that allowed Jewish exiles in Persia to return to Jerusalem to rebuild the temple (538 BC). During this time, the united kingdom of Israel and Judah divided (931 BC). As a result of their disobedience to God's laws and covenants, Israel went into Assyrian captivity (722 BC) and Judah into Babylonian captivity (587 BC).

5. **Development of Message**

    2 Chronicles tells about God's faithfulness in keeping His covenant promises to David. Its message develops through a focus on the worship of God. It tells about the temple, Levites, priests, and ways to worship *(20:18-22)*. It tells about the building of Solomon's temple *(2:1-8:16)*, and the ministry of the temple *(20:5-13, 24-30; 24:4-14)*.

6. **Theology**

    2 Chronicles shows how God keeps His covenant promises through preserving David's descendants *(6:14-17; 22:10-23:3)*. It also shows the importance of David's descendants obeying and worshiping God in response to God's mercy and faithfulness (see *7:4-7; 23:16-21*). Once again, obedience to God would bring blessings, while disobedience would bring consequences *(7:12-22)*.

7. Uniqueness and How to Preach It in Your Church Plant

2 Chronicles emphasizes how important prayer is in our relationship with God. It has several examples of prayer *(6:12-42; 30:18-20; 32:20-22)*. It also has God's advice regarding prayer in times of need *(7:12-16)*. Preach that prayer is important in the life of every believer *(Luk. 18:1)*. Jesus' disciples asked Him to teach them about prayer *(Luk. 11:1-4)*. Prayer should be a continual part of life for followers of Jesus *(1 The. 5:17; Phi. 4:6)*.

Assignment:

2 Chronicles shows that God kept His promises to David's descendants. God also warned them about their need to be obedient. Read *2 Chronicles 7:12-22*. In the space provided list the promises and warnings God made to Solomon, along with the verse numbers where the promises and warnings are found.

8. Outline of 2 Chronicles

A. Solomon's Reign *(1:1-9:31)*.
- Solomon's Wisdom and Wealth *(1:1-17)*.
- The Temple *(2:1-7:22)*.
- Solomon's Kingdom *(8:1-9:31)*.

B. History of the Kings of Judah *(10:1-36:23)*.
- The United Kingdom Divides *(10:1-11:23)*.
- Judah's Kings from Rehoboam to Zedekiah *(12:1-36:14)*.
- The Exile *(36:15-21)*.
- Cyrus' Edict *(36:22-23)*.

> NOTES

Chapter 15
Ezra

1. Introduction and Title

A. The book of Ezra tells about God fulfilling His promises to bring His people back from exile and rebuild Jerusalem and the temple. There is also an emphasis towards God's covenant with David. Ezra was originally one book with Nehemiah. These books record the last events of the Old Testament period.

B. This book is named for Ezra, a priest who was an expert on the Law of Moses *(7:6)*. Ezra led a group of Jewish exiles from Babylon to Jerusalem to help rebuild the temple, the city, and the Jewish community.

2. Authorship and Date

A. Ezra is generally believed to be the work of Ezra, for whom the book is named.

B. Ezra was probably written shortly after 450 BC.

3. Purpose, Themes & Structure

A. The purpose of Ezra is to remind the returned Jewish exiles to practice true worship and true obedience to God. It also shows God's faithfulness and how He restored the people to their land.

B. The theme of Ezra is restoration. The temple in Jerusalem needed to be restored *(chapters 1-6)*, as did the returning Jewish exiles *(chapters 7-10)*.

C. Ezra is structured as follows:
- The first section of the book *(chapters 1-6)* tells about restoring the temple.
- The second section of the book *(chapters 7-10)* tells about restoring the people.
  ▶ There is a 57-year gap between *chapters 6* and *7*.

4. Historical Background

Ezra tells about the first two returns of exiles from Babylon, which had been conquered by Persia. Unlike Babylon, Persia encouraged the people it conquered to practice their own religions. In order for the Jews to do that, they needed to restore Jerusalem and the temple there. So Persia's king Cyrus encouraged the Jews in Babylon to return to Jerusalem and settle there again. The first return was led by Zerubbabel in 538 BC (see *chapters 1-6*). These exiles worked hard to restore the temple and temple worship. The second return was led by Ezra in 458 BC (see *chapters 7-10*). Along with the prophets Haggai and

Zechariah *(6:14)*, Ezra worked to help all the Jewish exiles obey God and to honor His mercy and faithfulness.

5. Development of Message

Ezra was an encouragement to the Jerusalem community of exiles who had returned under Zerubbabel and Ezra. It showed that as the people of God rebuilt the temple *(chapter 3)*, God wanted to rebuild their hearts. He would build in them the kind of faith that would joyfully obey and honor His covenants and laws *(chapter 6)*.

6. Theology

Ezra shows that God will completely restore His people when they come back to Him *(chapters 9-10)*. This means that His people must turn away from their sin and follow God *(10:1-4)*. Once again, God is faithful to His promises to restore both Jerusalem and His people.

7. Uniqueness and How to Preach It in Your Church Plant

The book of Ezra shows the consequences of not keeping away from things that God warns against *(9:10-15)*. For the exiles, their disobedience led to their taking part in actions that God hated. Preach the rewards of staying away from bad influences. Bad company corrupts good character *(9:12; 1 Cor. 15:33)*. Preach that there are still things that God wants His people to stay away from (see *Col. 3:5-10; 1 The. 4:3-7; Pro. 11:1; Exo. 20:1-17*). Preach that even when we sin, if we repent God is faithful to forgive us *(1 Joh. 1:6-9)*.

Assignment:

Read *Ezra 9*. In the space below, write down God's blessings that Ezra remembers in his prayer with the verse numbers where you find them.

NOTES

8. Outline of the Book of Ezra

A. God's Temple Restored *(1:1-6:22)*.
- Zerubabbel Leads the First Return of Exiles *(1:1-2:70)*.
    ▶ Cyrus' Decree *(1:1-11)*.
    ▶ Census of the Returning Exiles *(2:1-70)*.
- Rebuilding the Temple *(3:1-6:22)*.
    ▶ Rebuilding Begins *(3:1-13)*.
    ▶ Rebuilding Delayed *(4:1-24)*.
    ▶ Rebuilding Completed *(5:1-6:22)*.

B. God's People Reformed *(7:1-10:44)*.
- Ezra Leads the Second Return of Exiles *(7:1-8:36)*.
    ▶ Artaxerxes' Decree *(7:1-28)*.
    ▶ Census of the Returning Exiles *(8:1-36)*.
- Reforming the People *(9:1-10:44)*.
    ▶ Ezra's Prayer *(9:1-15)*.
    ▶ The People Repent *(10:1-44)*.

Chapter 16
Nehemiah

1. Introduction and Title

A. The book of Nehemiah tells about the rebuilding of Jerusalem's walls after the Jewish exiles returned from Babylon. Nehemiah was originally one book with the book of Ezra.

B. The book is named for Nehemiah (the Jewish cupbearer to the Persian king), who led the return of Jewish exiles to their homeland. Nehemiah led the project of rebuilding the flattened walls of Jerusalem, and rebuilding the community of God's people.

2. Authorship and Date

A. Ezra, the priest, is often given credit for compiling the book of Nehemiah from a collection of Nehemiah's writings *(Ezr. 1:1)*.

B. The book of Nehemiah is about the third return of Jewish exiles from Persia in 444 BC. Nehemiah's first term as governor in Jerusalem lasted twelve years *(5:14)*, ending when he returned to Babylon *(13:6)*. Nehemiah's second term as governor probably began before 424 BC. The book is compiled from Nehemiah's eyewitness accounts. As a result it was probably written between 430 and 420 BC.

3. Purpose, Themes & Structure

A. Nehemiah's purpose is to show that God not only desired to rebuild the walls of Jerusalem, but also His people.

B. The overall theme of the Book of Nehemiah is restoration. Through Nehemiah, God restores the walls of Jerusalem, His people, and the covenant.

C. The structure of the Book of Nehemiah is built on two major sections:
- Rebuilding Jerusalem's walls *(chapters 1-7)*.
- The renewal of God's people *(chapters 8-13)*.

4. Historical Background

The Persian king Artaxerxes allowed Nehemiah to go to Jerusalem and rebuild its walls in 444 BC. The book of Nehemiah is set mostly in Jerusalem. This is seen as Nehemiah leads the Jewish exiles from Persia in rebuilding Jerusalem's walls and then renewing their covenant with God. It covers the nineteen years from 444-425 BC. Nehemiah returned to Persia in 432 BC, and returned to Jerusalem for the final time around 425 BC *(13:6)*.

NOTES

5. Development of Message

The message of the book of Nehemiah follows the theme of restoration. First, the walls of Jerusalem are restored *(chapters 1-7)*. That task takes just 52 days. Then, the people of God are restored *(chapters 8-13)*, a task that takes much longer.
- This book would have been a great encouragement and challenge for the exiles who had returned to Jerusalem to be faithful in worship and life. Even people who had opposed the rebuilding of Jerusalem would have to admit that restoring the walls had been a miracle of God *(6:16)*.

6. Theology

Nehemiah tells about the covenant between God and His people. God shows His faithfulness to the covenant through the success in rebuilding Jerusalem's walls. The success or failure of God's people depends upon their faithfulness to the covenant. It is important that Nehemiah leads the people through a ceremony that renews their covenant with God *(9:1-10:39)*. This covenant reminds the Jews what they must do. After years of exile in a foreign land, they must move forward as the people of God.
- The book of Nehemiah demonstrates God's patience and love as His people decide whether or not to live in obedience to the covenant.

7. Uniqueness and How to Preach It in Your Church Plant

The book of Nehemiah demonstrates how important a godly leader can be. Had Nehemiah only been concerned with rebuilding the walls of Jerusalem, he would have been done with his task in less than two months. Yet, God had also given Nehemiah the task of rebuilding His people. Leading them back into a full covenant relationship with God required years.
- Preach how Nehemiah was used by God to rebuild His people through:
    - Prayer *(1:4-11)*.
    - Planning *(2:6-8)*.
    - Protection *(4:9-23)*.
    - Promoting unity *(5:10-11)*.
    - Integrity *(6:1-13)*.

Assignment:

Find three examples in the book of Nehemiah that show Nehemiah was a godly leader. Write the verse numbers and the examples below.

1)

2)

3)

8. Outline of Nehemiah[15]

- A. Rebuilding the Walls *(1:1-6:19)*.
  - Nehemiah's Prayer *(1:1-11)*.
  - Planning for Jerusalem *(2:1-20)*.
  - Work on the Walls *(3:1-32)*.
  - Opposition to the Walls *(4:1-23)*.
  - Conflict among God's People *(5:1-19)*.
  - The Opposition Renews *(6:1-14)*.
  - The Walls Rebuilt *(6:15-19)*.

- B. Restoring God's People *(7:1-13:31)*.
  - Registry of the People *(7:1-73)*.
  - The Covenant Renewed and Revival *(8:1-10:39)*.
  - Jerusalem Repopulates *(11:1-12:26)*.
  - The Walls Dedicated to God *(12:27-47)*.
  - The People Restored *(13:1-31)*.

NOTES

Chapter 17
Esther

1. **Introduction and Title**

    A. The book of Esther is a wonderful story of God's care for His people while they were under Persian rule. It tells of the bravery of a young Jewish woman, Esther, who stands up for her people at a time when they face destruction.

    B. The book is named for its main character, Esther.

2. **Authorship and Date**

    A. The author of the book of Esther is unknown. Some think that Ezra or Nehemiah may have written it, but there is no specific evidence to indicate either of them as the author.

    B. Although some critics place the writing of Esther at a much later date, many scholars tend to place the date of Esther's writing around 465 BC.

3. **Purpose, Themes & Structure**

    A. The purpose of Esther was to remind the returned Jewish exiles that God was faithful to keep His promises to Israel.

    B. The key theme in Esther is God's covenant loyalty to Israel, even in a land that did not fear God or care about the Jews.

    C. The book of Esther is structured in two sections: the threat to the Jews *(1-5)*, and the triumph of the Jews *(6-10)*.

4. **Historical Background**

    A. Esther tells about a ten-year period (483-473 BC) during the reign of Xerxes. Xerxes had just come to Shushan (one of the four Persian capitals), after suffering defeat at the hands of the Greeks. It was during this period that Esther, a young Jewish woman, became his bride. Scholars suggest that these events fit between *chapters 6* and *7* of the book of Ezra.

    B. The book of Esther is also the only place in the Bible that tells about the many Jews who chose to remain in Persia rather than to return to Palestine.

5. **Development of Message**

    The message of the book of Esther is how God's providence can work to turn trouble into favor. It begins with Esther and the Jews being at risk in a strange land. The early part of the book *(chapters 1-5)*, explains the threats they faced.

Yet, it also shows the many ways God worked to keep His people safe. Later in the story *(chapters 6-10)*, God had brought about changes that not only removed the threats to His people, but also made them favored in Persia.

6. Theology

The book of Esther is unusual in that the name of God or even the word for "God" is not mentioned. This could be because the author believed the Jewish people who stayed in Persia (and did not return to Palestine *[Ezr. 1:1]*), were cut off from many of God's blessings. Yet, the very strong theological theme in Esther is God's providence and protection for His people. Esther is filled with evidence of God working.
- Esther is in the right place at the right time to be chosen as queen *(2:5-18)*.
- Mordecai is where he needs to be to interrupt a plot to kill the king *(2:19-23)*.
- The king reads the account of Mordecai's deed at the right time *(6:1-3)*.

7. Uniqueness and How to Preach It in Your Church Plant

The book of Esther gives a special opportunity to preach about the impact of personal decisions. During the time that the Jews in Persia are threatened with destruction, the Jewish people need Esther to tell the king that she is also Jewish. Mordecai reminds Esther that she may be in her position as queen to save the Jewish people in Persia from death *(4:14)*. He challenges Esther to tell the king that a royal decree to kill the Jews in Persia would mean her death, too.
- Preach that there are times when every believer is in the right place at the right time to share the Gospel. Though it may not always be clear, God is always at work around us. We must remember that through our witness we are responsible to spare others from eternal destruction *(Jude 20-23)*.

Assignment:

God is not named in this book, but you can still see Him at work. Find two places in the book of Esther where it is clear to you that God is working on behalf of His people. Write down the verse numbers and the events below.

1)

2)

NOTES

8. Outline of Esther

A. The Jews in Trouble *(1:1-4:17)*.
- The Feast and the Divorce *(1:1-22)*.
- Xerxes Chooses Esther *(2:1-23)*.
- Haman Plots to Destroy Mordecai and the Jews *(3:1-15)*.
- Mordecai Challenges Esther *(4:1-17)*.

B. The Jews Triumph *(5:1-10:3)*.
- Esther's Success *(5:1-7:10)*.
- Haman Falls, the Jews Are Delivered *(8:1-9:16)*.
- The Feast of Purim *(9:17-32)*.
- Mordecai's Fame *(10:1-3)*.

Chapter 18
Job

1. Introduction and Title

   A. The book of Job is the one of five Poetry books in the Old Testament. The others are Psalms, Proverbs, Ecclesiastes and Song of Solomon.

   B. Job covers a question almost everyone asks: "Why does God allow suffering?" The book of Job shows that this question is too big for us. Yet, Job's story can help us understand God's view on suffering.

2. Authorship and Date

   A. Some think the writer of the book of Job was Job. Others think that Elihu (the fourth friend in this book), Solomon, or Moses wrote this book.

   B. If Job is the author, then the book could have been written around 2150 BC. This would make Job the oldest book in the Bible.[16]

3. Purpose, Themes & Structure

   A. The purpose of Job is to teach that God is in control even when the righteous suffer.

   B. The theme of Job is what Job learns through his suffering: God is the supreme ruler over the entire universe, including our lives, regardless of our situation.

   C. The structure of the Book of Job is in three parts.
   - The first part describes Job's life before and entering into his suffering *(chapters 1-2)*.
   - The second part is made up of the talks between Job and his friends *(chapters 3-37)*.
   - The third section is God's answer to Job and his suffering *(chapters 38-42)*, and also tells about the remainder of Job's life.

4. Historical Background

Job is set in the time of the patriarchs. It tells that Job's wealth is measured in livestock *(1:3; 42:12)*. It says that the Sabeans and Chaldeans are wandering raiders *(1:15, 17)*. The word used for "piece of silver" is used only here *(42:11)*, and in talking about Jacob *(Gen. 33:19; Jos. 24:32)*. These all indicate that Job's life is set in the time of the patriarchs (around 2200 -1800 BC).

5. Development of Message

Job's message begins by telling that Job is a righteous man *(1:1-5)*. The book continues with a talk between Satan and God *(1:6-2:13)*. Satan tells God that Job would no longer be righteous if God would allow Job to suffer. God says He is sure Job would continue to be righteous, and allows Satan to bring suffering to Job's life. In fact, God initiated the discussion with Satan. As Job suffers, his friends are certain that Job has sinned to cause such suffering. This begins a series of debates between Job and his friends about suffering and what it means *(3:1-37:24)*. During these talks, Job's friends say that his suffering means he has sinned. Job says he is innocent, and begins to talk about God as though God could be blamed for injustice. God answers Job with questions of His own *(38:1-41:34)*. Job repents and God restores him and his wealth *(42:1-17)*.

6. Theology

The book of Job shows that God is completely free to do what He wants, and also completely good *(38:1-41:34)*. This means that God, who controls nature *(36:1-37:24)*, is not controlled by human actions. He does not have to punish or reward anyone. Our suffering is not necessarily connected to our sin or our goodness. Sometimes the innocent suffer. Yet, whether we are suffering or not, we must faithfully accept that God's plan for us is good *(42:1-6; Jam. 5:11)*. He is good and He is free, that is what Job loudly proclaims to us.

7. Uniqueness and How to Preach It in Your Church Plant

A. Job shows how important it is to trust God, especially when we face troubles *(42:1-6)*. No one likes to suffer. Yet God is still worthy of our love and worship. We may not understand it, but He always has a plan when He allows suffering.

B. Preach that God can draw us closer to Him when we suffer *(Phi. 3:7-11)*. Preach that suffering for doing good is commendable before God *(1 Pet. 2:19-24)*. When we go through suffering with the right attitude, God builds His character in us *(Rom. 5:1-5)*.
- Prosperity is not always granted when we follow after God. Not every story ends happily. The majority of people who followed God in the New Testament did not end with prosperity, but with persecution and suffering.

Assignment:

Look at God's responses to Job in *38:1-40:2* and *40:6-41:34*. Find three statements God makes to show He is the Ruler over everything. Write the statements and where you found them in the space provided.

1)

2)

3)

8. Outline of the Book of Job

A. Job's Problem *(1:1-2:13)*.
   - Job's Good Life *(1:1-5)*.
   - Satan Attacks Job's Integrity *(1:6-22)*.
   - Satan Attacks Job's Health *(2:1-10)*.
   - Job's Friends Arrive *(2:11-13)*.

B. Job and His Friends Debate *(3:1-37:24)*.
   - The First Round *(3:1-14:22)*.
     - ▶ Job's Case *(3:1-26)*.
     - ▶ Eliphaz and Job *(4:1-7:21)*.
     - ▶ Bildad and Job *(8:1-10:22)*.
     - ▶ Zophar and Job *(11:1-14:22)*.
   - The Second Round *(15:1-21:34)*.
     - ▶ Eliphaz and Job *(15:1-17:16)*.
     - ▶ Bildad and Job *(18:1-19:29)*.
     - ▶ Zophar and Job *(20:1-21:34)*.
   - The Third Round *(22:1-26:14)*.
     - ▶ Eliphaz and Job *(22:1-24:25)*.
     - ▶ Bildad and Job *(25:1-26:14)*.
   - Job Defends Himself *(27:1-31:40)*.
   - Elihu Speaks *(32:1-37:24)*.

C. Job Restored *(38:1-42:17)*.
   - God Restores Job and Corrects His Friends *(42:7-17)*.

Chapter 19
Psalms

1. Introduction and Title

A. The book of Psalms is often called the heart of the Old Testament. It is a collection of individual poems that were meant to be sung with instrumental music. The poems tell about many different kinds of life experiences. Each of them offers some kind of praise or prayer to God. Parts of the book of Psalms were used as a song book in ancient Israel for their worship services.

B. The title of the book of Psalms is taken from the Greek Old Testament (the Septuagint), which called the book *Psalmoi*.

2. Authorship and Date

A. The Psalms have a number of different authors. In about two-thirds of the 150 psalms, the author's name is listed before the psalm he wrote. David is the author of 75 psalms. Moses wrote at least one psalm. Solomon wrote two psalms. Some of the men David put in charge of worship in Israel while he was king (Ethan, Heman, and Asaph) wrote psalms in this book. A group of musicians called the Sons of Korah wrote ten psalms in the collection. There are 50 psalms without a listed author. Some of them may have been written by Ezra, but most of the authors are unknown.

B. The dates of the individual psalms range nearly 1,000 years from 1410-430 BC. The book of Psalms was probably put together as we know it around 450-425 BC in the days of Ezra and Nehemiah in Jerusalem.

3. Purpose, Themes & Structure

A. The purpose of Psalms is to lead people into the worship, praise and confession of the one true God.

B. There are a variety of themes in the Psalms.
- "Lament psalms" are prayers by individuals or groups for God to deliver them. Some examples are: *Psalms 3-7, 13, 25-28, 80, 120*.
- "Thanksgiving psalms" are praise songs that thank God for His blessings. Some examples are: *Psalms 8, 29, 32-34, 66, 124, 139, 146-148*.
- "Enthronement psalms" tell about God's mighty rule over all His creation. Some examples are: *Psalms 47, 93, 96-99*.
- "Pilgrimage psalms" were sung by people on the way to Jerusalem for Jewish festivals. Some examples are: *Psalms 43, 48, 84, 120-134*.
- "Royal psalms" tell about the earthly king as well as God. Some examples are: *Psalms 2, 18, 20, 45, 89, 132*.

- "Wisdom psalms" tell about wisdom, righteousness, and finding God's will. Some examples are: *Psalms 1, 37, 119*.
- "Imprecatory psalms" are prayers from people asking God to curse or cause harm to their enemies. Some examples are: *Psalms 35, 55, 79, 137, 144*.

C. With exception to the Song of Solomon, the book of Psalms is the only poetic collection in Scripture. Psalms is structured in five books. There are several ways to describe this structure. One way is to compare the content of the five books within the Psalms to the content of the five books of Moses *(Genesis-Deuteronomy)*.
- <u>Book One</u> *(Psalms 1-41)*, contains the overall topics of Genesis: man and creation.
- <u>Book Two</u> *(Psalms 42-72)*, tells about the overall topics of Exodus: rescue and redemption.
- <u>Book Three</u> *(Psalms 73-89)*, covers the topics of Leviticus: worship and holiness.
- <u>Book Four</u> *(Psalms 90-106)*, tells about the overall topics of Numbers: wilderness and wandering.
- <u>Book Five</u> *(Psalms 107-150)*, contains the overall topics of Deuteronomy: the Word of God and worship.

4. Historical Background

Psalms covers the time from Moses through the Jewish exiles' third return to Jerusalem. Because over half the psalms were written by David and other musicians of his time, most of the psalms are about that particular time in history (about 1020-970 BC).

5. Development of Message

The 150 Psalms each have their own message. Yet, all have a common point: to praise and honor God. The book begins and ends with songs of worship and praise that focus on God *(Psalms 1-41, 90-150)*. In the middle are psalms that tell why God is worthy of our praise and how we should give thanks in every situation *(Psalms 42-89)*.

6. Theology

A. The book of Psalms shows that God is worthy of praise and worship every moment and in every situation *(Psalm 150)*. Whether we find ourselves sad *(Psalm 22)*, joyful *(Psalm 27)*, giving thanks *(Psalm 136)*, or seeking forgiveness *(Psalm 51)*, God is always worthy of praise.

B. The heart of the Psalms (and the entire Old Testament) is the relationship between God and man. Psalms describes God in many different ways in His relationship towards man: as a shepherd, a warrior, a father, a king, a husband, a protector, and more. Each way emphasizes a particular aspect of God's relationship with His people.

NOTES

7. Uniqueness and How to Preach It in Your Church Plant

The book of Psalms shows how to connect almost every situation in life with a reason to worship God. Many psalms are examples of blessing God at all times *(34:1)*. Preach how important it is to find reasons to thank God *(92:1-2)*. Preach that God is worthy of our gifts and honor simply because He is God *(96)*. Preach that we must worship God from our hearts and in truth *(Joh. 4:21-24)*.

Assignment:

Pick five Psalms and read them. Then list the reasons to worship God that were found in each psalm.

1)

2)

3)

4)

5)

8. Outline of the Book of Psalms

    A. Book 1: Worship Songs by David, about Man and Creation *(1-41)*.

    B. Book 2: Personal and National Songs by David and Korah, about Rescue and Redemption *(42-72)*.

    C. Book 3: Personal and National Songs by Asaph, about Worship and Holiness *(73-89)*.

    D. Book 4: Praise Songs by Moses, David and Unknown Authors, about Wilderness and Wandering *(90-106)*.

    E. Book 5: Praise Songs by David and Unknown Authors, about the Word of God and Worship *(107-150)*.

Chapter 20
Proverbs

1. Introduction and Title

A. The book of Proverbs tells how faith in God and obedience to His Word is lived out in day-to-day life. It is a book that shows what God's wisdom looks like when it is put into action. Proverbs makes right and wrong conduct clear for many situations.
   - Proverbs is an example of wisdom literature in the Old Testament. Wisdom literature describes thoughts about life in memorable forms.
     ▶ <u>Proverbial wisdom literature</u> uses short statements that describe life with comparisons, parables, or sayings.
     ▶ <u>Speculative wisdom literature</u> uses stories to describe the basic problems of life such as the path to success, the problem of suffering, or the meaning of life.

B. The title for Proverbs comes from its Latin title: *Liber Proverbiorum*, which means "Book of Proverbs."

2. Authorship and Date

A. Solomon is responsible for about 800 of the sayings in the book of Proverbs. His name is above three sections in the book *(1-9; 10:1-22:16; 25-29)*. There are also sayings by Agur *(30:1-33)*, and King Lemuel *(31:1-9)*. The final section of Proverbs about the virtuous woman *(31:10-31)*, may have been written by Lemuel, but that is not certain.

B. The proverbs by Solomon would have been written before his death in 931 BC. Solomon's proverbs that Hezekiah's men compiled would have been written down around 700 BC. It is likely that the book of Proverbs was finally compiled around that date.[17]

3. Purpose, Themes & Structure

A. The purpose of Proverbs is to tell about the importance of a pure heart and a clear mind in order to act wisely in everyday life *(1:2-6)*.

B. The main theme of Proverbs is godly wisdom, which begins with the fear of the Lord *(9:10)*. Wisdom here means proper living according to God's Word and ways. In the book of Proverbs, someone who is wise is a person who knows and follows God's way.

C. The book of Proverbs is structured around seven sections of sayings or teachings.
   - The first section tells about the value of wisdom *(1-9)*.
   - The second section tells about wise living in many areas of life *(10:1-22:16)*.

- The third section contains sayings of wise men. It also addresses many areas of life *(22:17-24:34)*.
- The fourth section contains another collection of proverbs covering many areas of life *(25-29)*.
- The fifth section has wise sayings about honoring God and the value of hard work *(30)*.
- The sixth section has wise sayings about the dangers of strong drink, and the need to speak up for the needy *(31:1-9)*.
- The seventh section tells about a righteous wife *(31:10-31)*.

4. Historical Background

Most of Proverbs was written by Solomon in the time when he was the king of Israel (971-931 BC). Solomon had asked God for wisdom in ruling Israel, and God had given it to him *(2 Chr. 1:8-12)*. Solomon was known for his wisdom, and the Bible says he wrote 3,000 proverbs *(1 Kin. 4:32)*. Although these sayings were written long ago, the wisdom of this book applies as much today as when it was originally written.

5. Development of Message

The book of Proverbs develops its message by showing that the wisdom of God applies to every area of life. The sayings themselves cover a wide range of topics, including:
- Marriage *(5:18)*.
- Business *(16:11)*.
- Parenthood *(19:18)*.

6. Theology

The theology of Proverbs sets it apart from other ancient collections of wisdom sayings. The entire book is based on the truth that the fear of God is where wisdom begins (1:7). Wisdom is not achieved by living for many years, or by knowing many things. Wisdom is only possible by knowing and honoring God first. Fearing God is a motif that much of Scripture is built around. Paul continues this motif in the New Testament.

7. Uniqueness and How to Preach It in Your Church Plant

A. The book of Proverbs has a special passage that points toward Jesus Christ.[18] *Proverbs 8:22-31* says: *"wisdom was present with God from before the beginning of creation… wisdom was beside God as an expert craftsman as God created all things."* *John 1:1* reminds us that the Word was in the beginning, was with God, and was God. Nothing was made without the Word, Who is Jesus Christ.

B. Remind people that God wants to apply His wisdom to our lives *(Col. 1:9-11)*. God gives wisdom to those who will listen to and obey it *(Pro. 2:1-9)*. Preach that Jesus Christ is the Wisdom of God made flesh *(1 Cor. 1:30-31; Col. 2:9)*. Christ holds the treasures of wisdom and knowledge *(Col. 2:2-3)*.

Assignment:

In the space below, list four proverbs about wise family living from the book of Proverbs.

1)

2)

3)

4)

8. Outline of the book of Proverbs

    A. Proverbs on the Value of Wisdom *(1:1-9:18)*.

    B. Three Collections of Proverbs about Wise Living *(10:1-29:27)*.

    C. Sayings about Honoring God, Righteous Choices and Hard Work *(30:1-33)*.

    D. Sayings about Strong Drink and Justice *(31:1-9)*.

    E. The Righteous Wife *(31:10-31)*.

NOTES

Chapter 21
Ecclesiastes

1. Introduction and Title

A. The book of Ecclesiastes tells about the search for meaning in life. It says that every area in life – work, wealth, wisdom, righteousness, and youth – is empty and temporary. It shows the limitations of human work and wisdom. Yet, Ecclesiastes also shows that when humans see their limitations, they can be free to live in the reverence and awe of God.

B. The title of Ecclesiastes comes from its Greek title *Ekklesiastes*. The word means "one who calls an assembly."

2. Authorship and Date

Scholars and tradition say that Solomon is the author of Ecclesiastes. The author of the book never names himself. Yet he calls himself: *a son of David (1:1)*, *a king in Jerusalem (1:2)*, and *king over Israel in Jerusalem (1:12)*. He also says he was wiser than anyone before him *(1:16)*, had great wealth, and a large harem *(2:8)*. This evidence within Ecclesiastes points to Solomon writing the book around 935 BC.

3. Purpose, Themes & Structure

A. The purpose of Ecclesiastes is to show the emptiness of every part of life without God. Some believe that Solomon may have written Ecclesiastes to teach other nations about their need for God.[19] Life is a vapor and this vapor comes and goes.

B. The theme of Ecclesiastes is that the search for life's meaning in human activity is worthless. Life has meaning only when we see it with God in the picture. The fear of the Lord is essential to godly living in this book. The Apostle Paul draws on the end of Ecclesiastes in 2 Corinthians 5. Solomon understood the reality of the believer standing before God for an evaluation of his or her life.

C. Ecclesiastes is structured with:
   - An introduction *(1:1-11)*.
   - Teaching about the limitations of human work and wisdom *(1:12-11:6)*.
   - Advice to fear God and keep His commandments *(11:7-12:14)*.

4. Historical Background

Ecclesiastes tells about the lessons Solomon learned during his life. It is set in Judah. Many believe that Solomon wrote Ecclesiastes near the end of his life.

5. Development of Message

The message of Ecclesiastes develops in two stages. First, the book shows how empty life can be when people try to satisfy themselves with work, wealth, and human wisdom *(1:1-11:6)*. Life is a vapor and therefore it is fleeting. Then the book tells us people should live with joy and integrity, with complete trust in God *(11:7-12:14)*.

6. Theology

The theology in Ecclesiastes says that God created mankind with eternity in our hearts *(3:11)*. This helps explain the feelings of emptiness that result from living as though human activity is all there is to life *(2)*. For life to be fulfilling, we need to understand that human effort and human wisdom are limited in every way. We must see that life is a gift from God *(3:12-13)*. To live well, we must live in the understanding that we must obey and honor God *(12:13-14)*.

7. Uniqueness and How to Preach It in Your Church Plant

A. Ecclesiastes gives us Solomon's insight on life. The wisest man in the world had wealth, power and all the pleasure he wanted *(2:1-10)*. Yet it wasn't enough *(2:11)*. It was all empty unless God was given His right place *(2:26)*.

B. Preach that many things that seem good are only temporary. Popularity *(4:13)*, wealth and honor *(5:8-17)*, are among those things. God gives joy in many things this life has to offer *(5:18-20)*, but only when people see the life they have as a gift from God *(2:24; 3:12-13)*.

Assignment:

Read *Ecclesiastes 4-6*. Pick three verses or passages from those chapters, and tell about the advice they offer in the spaces below.

1)

2)

3)

8. Outline of Ecclesiastes

A. The Vapor of Life *(1:1-11)*.

B. The Vapor of Human Activity *(1:12-6:9)*.

C. The Vapor of Human Wisdom *(6:10-11:6)*.

D. Good Advice: Live in Joy and Reverence before God *(11:7-12:7)*.

E. Fear God and Keep His Commandments *(12:8-14)*.

Chapter 22
Song of Solomon

1. Introduction and Title

A. Song of Solomon (also known as Song of Songs) is a collection of love poems and songs. The book shows that love, including sexual love, within marriage is a gift from God. It also shows how love within a faithful marriage grows and matures.

B. The title of the book comes from its literary form (songs), and from its author Solomon.

2. Authorship and Date

A. Song of Solomon itself says that Solomon is its author. Scholars and tradition agree.

B. Scholars believe that Solomon wrote this book early in his kingship with his first wife being "The Shulamite" in the Song of Solomon. This would place the book's writing sometime around 971 BC.

3. Purpose, Themes & Structure

A. The purpose of Song of Solomon is to commend sexual love between a man and woman in marriage. Some early scholars also saw Song of Solomon as an illustration of the love of God for Israel, or the love of Christ for the church. Yet the Scriptures give no evidence that would make the book any less about human marriage.

B. The theme of Song of Solomon is human love that can be blessed and celebrated in a godly relationship.

C. The structure of Song of Solomon is that of a lyric idyll.[20] This type of love song features speeches or small poems that may not appear to be in order. It also has a chorus that helps move the song from one speech or poem to the next.

4. Historical Background

Song of Solomon takes place in the early years of King Solomon's rule (971-931 BC). It describes the romance between Solomon and his first bride, called "The Shulamite," who came from a place near Ball Hamon in the northernmost part of Galilee.[21]

NOTES

5. Development of Message

The message develops in Song of Solomon as the romance between King Solomon and his beloved progresses from courtship *(1:1-3:5)*, to their wedding *(3:6-5:1)*. The story goes on to tell about the couple's marriage *(5:2-8:4)*. Then the book describes the nature and power of love *(8:5-14)*.

6. Theology

Song of Solomon provides a proper biblical balance to the essential goodness and rightness of physical love within the God-given framework of marriage.
- God created man and woman *(Gen. 1:17; 2:20-23)*. He also established marriage *(Gen. 2:24)*. Marriage is very important to God. Song of Solomon gives an example of what a marriage that honors God can look like.

7. Uniqueness and How to Preach It in Your Church Plant

The Song of Solomon warns about the need to keep sexually pure before marriage. To do this, it uses the phrase *Do not stir up or awaken love until it pleases*, which is found only within marriage *(2:7; 3:5; 8:4)*. Song of Solomon also says that sexual love within marriage is wonderful *(4:1-6, 16)*. Preach that sexual love is a gift to be saved for marriage *(Heb. 13:4; Pro. 5:18-20)*. Today as in Solomon's time, God's will is to avoid sexual sin *(1 Cor. 6:18)*.
- Sex is a topic avoided by many in the church today. However, it is a gift given from God to man. Husband and wife are to enjoy each other within the biblical parameters of marriage. Various cultures downplay this discussion at all within life and the church. However, the Word of God sees the sexual relationship between a husband and wife as that which is holy and designed by Him.

Assignment:

Read *Song of Solomon 8:6-7*. Write down the three ways love is described in these verses. What do these verses say about the power of love?

1)

2)

3)

8. Outline of the Song of Solomon[22]

A. The Courtship *(1:1-3:5)*.

B. The Wedding *(3:6-5:1)*.

C. The Marriage and Recommitment *(5:2-8:4)*.

D. The Power of Love and How It Began *(8:5-14)*.

Chapter 23
Isaiah

1. Introduction and Title

A. The book of Isaiah is the first of sixteen books of the prophets in the Old Testament. It is also one of the books of the *Four Major Prophets* (Isaiah, Jeremiah, Ezekiel and Daniel). The *Major Prophets* are given that name not because of their importance, but because of the length of their books in the Bible.

B. Isaiah tells about Isaiah's life and his prophecies. God called Isaiah to a long prophetic ministry. Isaiah spoke from Jerusalem to several groups and nations over a 60-year period (from about 740-680 BC). The book of Isaiah also contains more prophecies about the Messiah than any other Old Testament book except the Psalms.

C. The book of Isaiah is named for the prophet it tells about. Isaiah's name means *Salvation is of the Lord*.

2. Authorship and Date

A. The prophet Isaiah wrote the book of Isaiah.

B. The book was compiled throughout Isaiah's life as a prophet (740 – 680 BC).

3. Purpose, Themes & Structure

A. The purposes of Isaiah were to remind God's people of their special relationship with God as a part of His covenant, and to call the nation of Judah back to God.

B. The general theme of Isaiah is that salvation comes from the Lord; and those who follow obediently after God will experience that salvation one day.

C. The book of Isaiah is structured around the themes in the book.
- Judgment is pronounced on the eighth-century Israelites of the united kingdom of Judah and Israel, then on a number of nations *(1-36)*.
- Between the major themes is the story of Hezekiah *(37-39)*.
- Isaiah then offers comfort and restoration to God's covenant people through the present activity of God and the coming Messiah *(40-66)*.

4. Historical Background

According to *Isaiah 1:1*, Isaiah was active from a date near the end of Uzziah's time in power (about 740 BC), through the reigns of Jotham (739-731

BC), Ahaz (731-715 BC), and Hezekiah (715-686 BC). Assyria was a powerful nation in the region early in Isaiah's ministry, and took over the Northern Kingdom of Israel in 722 BC. Israel and Judah found themselves in a time of prosperity, greed, indulgence and injustice for most of Isaiah's ministry.

5. Development of Message

The message in Isaiah develops in a way that shows how judgment will be the path that leads to forgiveness and restoration. The book begins with judgment for rebellion and sin *(1-39)*. It then tells about sin being forgiven and the changes that follow *(40-66)*.

6. Theology

A. God's names show His kingship.[23] Of special importance in Isaiah is "The Holy One of Israel," which occurs 25 times in the book. This title emphasizes God's greatness and perfection, which is the core of Isaiah's theology.
  - Isaiah's understanding of God is rooted in the vision he received of God at the beginning of his ministry *(6)*.
    ▶ It shows God's greatness and perfection in character *(6:1)*.
    ▶ It shows God's moral perfection when compared to man *(6:5)*.
    ▶ It demonstrates God's gracious relationship with Israel, a sinful people *(6:7)*.
  - Isaiah's theology made him see that God must be exalted: God is the true king *(6:1; 12:6; 33:15-16)*.
  - Isaiah's theology made him see that man must be humbled. Israel's main sin is that they have put man in the place of God and God in the place of man *(2:11-18; 10:20; 17:7; 31:1)*.

B. Isaiah also shows that God is active in history and all of His creation. He is constantly putting events into motion among His people and the nations *(9:8-10:12; 19:1-6; 45:1-13)*.

7. Uniqueness and How to Preach It in Your Church Plant

A. Of all the prophetic books in the Old Testament, Isaiah has the largest number of messianic prophecies. The book of Isaiah tells about:
  - Christ's birth to a virgin *(Isa. 7:14; Luk. 1:26-31)*.
  - His miracles *(Isa. 35:5-6; Mat. 12:22; Luk. 4:18; 7:22)*.
  - His obedience *(Isa. 50:5; Mat. 26:39)*.
  - His message *(Isa. 61:1-2; Luk. 4:18-19)*.
  - His suffering and death *(Isa. 50:6; 53:1-12; Mat. 27:26, 30)*.
  - His exaltation *(Isa. 52:13; Rom. 4:24-25; Phi. 2:9-11)*.

B. You can find the fulfillment of each of these prophecies and others in the New Testament. Preach that Jesus fulfills these prophecies about the Messiah as no one else could have done. Show the connection between the prophecies in Isaiah and the places in the New Testament, like those listed above that tell how Jesus fulfilled them.

NOTES

> ### Assignment:
>
> Find at least three different names for God in the book of Isaiah. List the names and the verse numbers where you find them below.
>
> 1)
>
> 2)
>
> 3)

8. Outline of Isaiah

- A. Judgment for Sin *(1-36)*.
    - Prophecies about Judah *(1:1-12:6)*.
    - Prophecies against the Nations *(13:1-23:18)*.
    - A Time of Judgment, then Triumph *(24:1-27:13)*.
    - Warnings and Woes *(28:1-33:24)*.
    - The Lord Repays and Blesses *(34:1-35:10)*.

- B. Hezekiah *(36-39)*.
    - God Saves Hezekiah from Assyria *(36:1-37:38)*.
    - God Heals Hezekiah *(38:1-22)*.
    - Hezekiah's Sin *(39:1-8)*.

- C. God's Redemption and Restoration *(40-66)*.
    - God Delivers His People *(40:1-48:22)*.
    - The Suffering Servant Brings Salvation *(49:1-57:21)*.
    - God's Restoration is Complete *(58:1-66:24)*.

Chapter 24
Jeremiah

1. Introduction and Title

A. The book of Jeremiah is filled with warnings to a people whose hearts were no longer set on God. Jeremiah tells about the last 50 years of Judah before they were conquered by Babylon. It is mostly a sad story, and the sadness of the priest and prophet Jeremiah for his people often shows in this book.

B. The title of this book comes from the name of the prophet Jeremiah, which probably means *The Lord Establishes*.

2. Authorship and Date

A. *Jeremiah 1:1* states that Jeremiah is the author of the book. Jeremiah's secretary Baruch wrote down Jeremiah's prophecies.

B. Jeremiah prophesied from about 627-580 BC. The book of Jeremiah was probably completed toward the end of this time period, after the fall of Jerusalem in 586 BC.

3. Purpose, Themes & Structure

A. The purpose of the book of Jeremiah was to remind Judah that disobedience to God's covenant would bring them disaster. Only a commitment to obeying God would save them from His judgment.

B. The theme of Jeremiah is God's judgment, first on Judah and then on the nations of the world.

C. Jeremiah is structured more on content than on the order of events in history. The book begins by telling about Jeremiah's call to ministry *(1:1-19)*. It continues with Jeremiah's prophecies of judgment against Judah *(2-45)*, and the nations of the world *(46-51)*. The book ends with a chapter that tells about the fall of Jerusalem to Babylon *(52)*.

4. Historical Background

A. Jeremiah based his ministry in Jerusalem. He prophesied from about 627-580 BC. For about 40 years, Jeremiah's message was that God would judge Judah for their rebellious ways. From 627-605 BC, Jeremiah spoke this message while Assyria and Egypt were a threat to Judah. Then from 605-586 BC, Jeremiah warned of God's judgment while Babylon prepared to conquer Judah. From 586 to about 580 BC, Jeremiah continued his work in Jerusalem and Egypt.

B. Jeremiah was alive at the same time as Ezekiel, Daniel, Habakkuk, and Zephaniah.

NOTES

5. Development of Message

The message of Jeremiah makes it clear that even though the people of Judah had access to worship in the temple and had the one true religion; they still needed to obey their covenant with God or face disaster.

6. Theology

Jeremiah shows that because of His great love and faithfulness, God is a God who restores. Jeremiah's message was one of judgment. Yet, it also told that God promised to bring His people back from exile and restore them *(30:18-31:6)*. These restored people would have God's covenant written on their hearts *(31:31-34)*. They would be people who lived in ways that showed God's character. All of this leads to the work of Jesus, His payment for sins, and the work of the Holy Spirit in the lives of true followers of Christ.

7. Uniqueness and How to Preach It in Your Church Plant

The book of Jeremiah shows that sometimes prophets struggled with the messages they had to give. Jeremiah cried when he thought about the judgment coming to his people *(9:1; 13:17; 14:17)*. He was unhappy about how people treated him for the message he spoke *(20:7-10)*. Yet, Jeremiah was faithful in speaking the message God had given him *(18:19-20)*. Preach that it is important to remain faithful to the message God gives us *(Rom. 1:15-17)*. Even though it may not be the message others want to hear, we need to speak the truth about Jesus Christ *(Act. 4:1-22)*.

Assignment:

Find two places in the book of Jeremiah where Jeremiah was mistreated by the people around him for speaking God's message. Then find two places where God encourages Jeremiah to stay faithful to His message. Write the verse numbers and a short description of these places below.

Mistreatment

1)

2)

Encouragement

1)

2)

8. Outline of the book of Jeremiah

A. Jeremiah's Call *(1:1-19)*.

B. Prophecies to Judah *(2:1-45:5)*.
- God's Judgment on Judah *(2:1-25:38)*.
- Jeremiah's Conflicts with Judah *(26:1-29:32)*.
- Future Restoration of Israel and Judah *(30:1-33:26)*.
- Jerusalem's Fall *(34:1-45:5)*.

C. Prophecies to the Nations *(46:1-49:39)*.

D. Prophecies against Babylon *(50:1-51:64)*.

E. Jerusalem's Fall Reviewed *(52:1-34)*.

Chapter 25
Lamentations

1. Introduction and Title

    A. The book of Lamentations shows the grief felt by the prophet Jeremiah when Jerusalem fell to Babylon. Where the book of Job is about personal suffering, the book of Lamentations is about the suffering of a nation (Judah).

    B. The title for Lamentations is taken from the first word in the book, which is a "lament" or expression of mourning.

2. Authorship and Date

    A. According to Jewish tradition and likenesses in style to the book of Jeremiah, the prophet Jeremiah is the author of Lamentations.

    B. Lamentations was written in Jerusalem. Because Jeremiah was in Jerusalem for just a short time after it fell to Babylon, the book was probably written in late 586 BC or early 585 BC.

3. Purpose, Themes & Structure

    A. The purpose of Lamentations was to show some of the reasons for, and results of, suffering. It also shows how God uses suffering for His purposes.

    B. The general theme in Lamentations is the faithfulness of God in difficult times.

    C. Lamentations is structured in five poems of sorrow called "dirges".

4. Historical Background

When Babylon destroyed Jerusalem in 586 BC, they killed many people and took many others into slavery. The survivors left in Jerusalem were in great sorrow not only for the loss of the city and its temple of worship, but also for the loss of their friends and families. Lamentations is a response to this tragedy.

5. Development of Message

    A. The Book of Lamentations has five chapters.
- The first two chapters describe the destruction of Jerusalem and the sadness of God's people.
- The third chapter tells about God's faithfulness.
- The fourth chapter tells that everyone left in Jerusalem is suffering.
- The final chapter is a prayer for restoration.

B. The message of Lamentations covers areas of sadness, praise and restoration.

6. Theology

Lamentations shows that God keeps His promises, even when those promises result in difficult consequences. In fact, Jeremiah says that God is faithful for bringing about hard consequences for Israel's disobedience *(3:22-33)*. This means that God will be just as faithful to restore the people of His covenant when the time is right *(5:21-22)*.

7. Uniqueness and How to Preach It in Your Church Plant

Lamentations states that God's faithfulness is sometimes seen in His judgment or anger *(3:22-33; 4:11-13)*. Preach that God's discipline shows that He cares *(Heb. 12:5-11; Rev. 3:19)*. Preach that God's discipline is righteous and meant to restore us *(Jer. 30:11-22)*.

Assignment:

Moses predicted the problems in the book of Lamentations in *Deuteronomy 28*. Read the passages from Lamentations below, and then match them to one of these three passages from Deuteronomy: *Deut. 28:50; Deut. 28:65; Deut. 28:41*.

1) *Lamentations 1:18*

2) *Lamentations 2:21*

3) *Lamentations 5:12*

8. Outline of Lamentations

    A. Jerusalem Destroyed Because of Its Sin *(1:1-22)*.

    B. God's Anger and Punishment of Jerusalem *(2:1-22)*.

    C. Jeremiah's Confession and Confidence *(3:1-66)*.

    D. Babylon Destroys Jerusalem *(4:1-22)*.

    E. Prayer for Restoration *(5:1-22)*.

Chapter 26
Ezekiel

1. Introduction and Title

A. The book of Ezekiel tells about the ministry of Ezekiel the prophet. Ezekiel was in the first group of Jewish exiles in Babylon. He preached to the exiled Jews at the same time Jeremiah was warning the remaining Jews in Jerusalem about the coming judgment against them.

B. The book of Ezekiel is named for Ezekiel the prophet. Ezekiel's name means *God Strengthens*.

2. Authorship and Date

A. The book of Ezekiel identifies its author as Ezekiel *(1:3; 24:24)*. Tradition and most scholars agree.

B. Ezekiel was written between the dates of Ezekiel's first vision (593-592 BC), and his last recorded vision (about 571-570 BC). This book is easily dated because Ezekiel was careful to include the dates of his visions as he wrote. The book of Ezekiel was probably finished shortly after 570 BC.

3. Purpose, Themes & Structure

A. The purpose of Ezekiel is to remind the exiles in Babylon that the God of the covenant had not forgotten them, even though they were far away from the temple and the Promised Land.

B. The theme of Ezekiel says that the purpose of God's grace and discipline is always to produce spiritual restoration in all people. In the book, this is given special notice with the phrase: *They shall know I am the Lord*.

C. The structure of Ezekiel is roughly the same as the book of Jeremiah.
   - Begins with the prophet's call *(1-3)*.
   - Ezekiel's first major section contains prophecies of judgment against Judah *(4-24)*.
   - Ezekiel's second section tells about God's judgment on the nations of the world *(25-32)*.
   - Ezekiel's third major section tells about the restoration of Judah *(33-48)*.

4. Historical Background

A. Ezekiel based his ministry in Babylon, where he was an exile. He prophesied between 592 BC and 570 BC, which was during the final fall of Judah to Babylon in 586 BC. The Babylonians settled the Jewish exiles near the Chebar River (in southeastern Iraq), to make them into a Babylonian colony. Ezekiel spoke God's message to these exiles in two stages. Before

Jerusalem fell in 586 BC, Ezekiel's message told about the coming judgment on Judah because of its sin. After Jerusalem fell, Ezekiel's message told about the future restoration of Jerusalem.

B. Ezekiel was alive at the same time as Jeremiah and Daniel.

5. Development of Message

The message of Ezekiel follows its structure. Judah would fall because of her disobedience to God *(3-24)*. The nations of the world would also be judged *(25-32)*. Yet, because God was faithful to the promises of His covenants with Israel, He would eventually restore His people *(33-48)*.

6. Theology

Ezekiel tells about God's glory and character. Ezekiel's ministry began with visions that demonstrated God's majesty and greatness *(1; 3:23)*. He often spoke about God's glory in the rest of the book *(8:4; 10:18-19; 39:11; 44:4)*. God's character is also important in Ezekiel's theology. Several times in Ezekiel, God says that He is acting on behalf of His name *(20:9, 14, 22, 39, 44; 36:20-23; 43:7-8)*. There are many times where God wants His character closely related to His actions so people would *"know that I am Lord" (6:7, 10, 13-14)*.[24]

7. Uniqueness and How to Preach It in Your Church Plant

A. Ezekiel shows that God cares about His people no matter where they are. The exiles in Babylon were hundreds of miles away from Jerusalem. They were supposed to forget about their lives in Judah and start new lives in Babylon. But God sent Ezekiel to let the exiles know that He had not turned His back on them and was still working *(3:1-21)*.

B. Preach that God wants to keep everyone aware of what He is doing, especially concerning Jesus. God made shepherds (that others often ignored), among the first to know of Jesus' birth *(Luk. 2:8-20)*. God made two elderly people, Simeon and Anna, among the first to see the baby Jesus *(Luk. 2:25-38)*. He brought the apostle Philip to an Ethiopian official so the official could understand the Good News about Jesus *(Act. 8:26-40)*. <u>Preach that everyone</u> (regardless of race, culture, caste, or tribe), <u>is within reach of the saving Gospel of Christ</u>.

> **NOTES**

> **Assignment:**
>
> Find three places other than those listed above where God says He is acting so people would know He is Lord. Write the action of God and its verse number in the spaces below.
>
> 1)
>
> 2)
>
> 3)

8. Outline of the book of Ezekiel[25]

    A. Ezekiel's Call *(1:1-3:27)*.

    B. God's Judgment on Judah *(4:1-24:27)*.

    C. God's Judgment on the Nations *(25:1-32:32)*.

    D. Israel Restored *(33:1-48:35)*.
- The New Temple *(40:1-43:27)*.
- The New Worship *(44:1-46:24)*.
- The New Order *(47:1-48:35)*.

Chapter 27
Daniel

1. Introduction and Title

A. The book of Daniel tells the story of Daniel, a Jewish exile who became a court official in Babylon. Daniel served as a close advisor to both the Babylonian king Nebuchadnezzar and to Cyrus, the Persian king who conquered Babylon.

B. The book of Daniel is named for Daniel, whose name means *God is My Judge*.

2. Authorship and Date

A. The book of Daniel names Daniel as its author (12:4). Tradition and many scholars agree.

B. Daniel was written by the ninth year of the Persian king Cyrus' reign (about 530 BC).

3. Purpose, Themes & Structure

A. The purpose of Daniel is to show how God works out His purposes even in a foreign land. Daniel has many important prophecies telling about how Gentile nations will affect Israel while Israel waits for the fulfillment of God's covenants. It also tells about Israel's place and blessing in the Millennial Age.

B. The themes in Daniel are God's faithfulness to His covenant even when His people were in exile; and God's authority over all nations.

C. Daniel is structured around the theme of God's authority over all nations, which is shown in two stages.
- The first stage tells about the future of the Gentile world powers *(2-7)*.
- The second stage tells about the future of the Jewish nation under the power of the Gentiles *(8-12)*.

4. Historical Background

A. Daniel's ministry took place from about 605-536 BC in Babylon. Daniel was from a noble Jewish family. As a youth, Daniel was taken from Jerusalem to Babylon in the first captivity in 605 BC. Once there, Daniel became a trusted advisor to Nebuchadnezzar, the king of Babylon who ruled from 605-562 BC. Persia conquered Babylon in 539 BC. Daniel once again became a prominent advisor to a foreign king, gaining favor with the Persians. The Persian king Cyrus decreed in 538 BC that the Jews in exile could return to Jerusalem and rebuild the temple and city there.

NOTES

B. Daniel lived at the same time as Ezekiel and Jeremiah.

5. Development of Message

The message of the book of Daniel develops in two ways.
- One way tells about the prophetic plans for the Gentiles *(2-7)*, and then narrows its focus to Israel in prophecy *(8-12)*.
- The second way shows how God protects those who keep His covenant without compromise *(1:8-16; 3:1-30; 6:4-24)*.

6. Theology

The book of Daniel shows God is the ruler of all nations. The events in every nation, both present and future, serve His purpose. The events surrounding Daniel, Shadrach, Meshach and Abednego's uncompromising obedience within Babylon served to show God's faithfulness to those who were faithful to Him. The events predicted in Daniel's prophecies show how God will bring events together to restore Israel.

7. Uniqueness and How to Preach It in Your Church Plant

The book of Daniel is a book with several examples that show obedience and great faith. Every such story is a good basis for a message. You can preach the example of Daniel, as a young man, refusing to eat from the king's table *(1:8-16)*. This story can encourage young people that obeying God can show others how to live better. The example of Shadrach, Meshach and Abednego shows that faith in God can even change the minds of kings *(3:1-30)*. The story of Daniel facing the lion's den shows that a strong faith can bring powerful results *(6:1-28)*. Preach that faith needs to grow every day, and that without it we can never please God *(Heb. 11:6)*.

Assignment:

Find four places in the book of Daniel that tell or show how God rewards faithful obedience. Write them in the spaces below, along with the verse numbers where you found them.

1)

2)

3)

4)

8. Outline of the Book of Daniel

A. Daniel's Personal History *(1:1-21)*.
- Daniel Taken from Judah *(1:1-7)*.
- Daniel's Faithfulness *(1:8-16)*.
- Daniel's Appointment *(1:17-21)*.

B. Prophetic History of the Gentiles *(2:1-7:28)*.
- Nebuchadnezzar's Dream *(2:1-49)*.
- Nebuchadnezzar's Image *(3:1-30)*.
- Nebuchadnezzar's Vision *(4:1-37)*.
- Belshazzar's Feast *(5:1-31)*.
- Darius' Orders *(6:1-28)*.
- Daniel's Vision of the Four Beasts *(7:1-28)*.

C. Prophetic Plan for Israel *(8:1-12:13)*.
- Daniel's Vision: The Ram and the Male Goat *(8:1-27)*.
- Daniel's Vision: The 70 Weeks *(9:1-27)*.
- Daniel's Vision: Israel's Future *(10:1-12:13)*.

Chapter 28
Hosea

1. Introduction and Title

A. When the prophet Hosea began his ministry, God told him to marry an unfaithful woman. Their marriage would show how Israel was unfaithful to God. The book of Hosea tells about Hosea's ministry in the northern kingdom of Israel in the years leading up to its fall to Assyria. It also tells about God's hatred of sin. Yet, as Hosea restores his wife Gomer, God gives him the message that Israel, too, would be restored.

B. The book of Hosea is named for the prophet Hosea, whose name means *Salvation*.

2. Authorship and Date

A. *Hosea 1:1* states that Hosea is the author.

B. It is believed that the book of Hosea was completed near the time Hosea finished his public ministry (about 710 BC).

3. Purpose, Themes & Structure

A. The purpose of Hosea was to condemn sin, warn Israel of God's coming judgment, and to remind the loyal people of God that His love would restore them.

B. The theme of Hosea is that Israel's covenant relationship with God is like a marriage. Like a marriage, both partners need to honor the covenant.

C. Hosea is structured as a story with two parts. The first part is the story of an unfaithful wife, Gomer, and her faithful husband Hosea *(1-3)*. The second part is the story of an unfaithful Israel and their faithful God *(4-14)*.

4. Historical Background

Hosea prophesied from about 755 BC to 710 BC in the northern kingdom of Israel. He was active in ministry starting in the final years of Jeroboam II (782-753 BC). He continued for six more kings of Israel through Hezekiah (732-722 BC), under whom Israel fell to Assyria. Hosea's ministry began with Israel in prosperity, but Israel declined as it fell into greater disobedience of God.

5. Development of Message

The message develops in Hosea according to the relationship between Hosea and his wife Gomer. This is followed by the relationship between God and Israel. The book first tells about the unfaithfulness of Gomer *(1:1-2:23)*, then how Hosea restores her *(3:1-5)*. The book then tells about the unfaithfulness and coming judgment of Israel *(4:1-10:15)*, and finally how God restores Israel *(11:1-14:9)*.

6. Theology

Hosea shows that God does not punish His people without a reason. In fact, Hosea shows that God's punishment is often the way He brings His people to their senses *(4:1-6:3)*. As God judges, His intent is to lead His people into redemption and restoration *(14:1-9)*.

7. Uniqueness and How to Preach It in Your Church Plant

The book of Hosea shows that God's love for mankind is often one-sided. Hosea shows that God loves His people faithfully, while His people often ignore Him or even reject Him *(11:1-12:14)*. Preach that God's love for us through Jesus Christ is also one-sided. While we were still sinners, ignoring and rejecting God, Christ died for us *(Rom. 5:8)*. God showed His love for us by sending Jesus. Even though God's love may be one-sided, there is still an expectation and requirement that we return His love. We love Him because He loved us first *(1 Joh. 4:9-10, 19)*.

Assignment:

Find four examples in the book of Hosea that tell about Hosea's love for his wife, or God's love for Israel. List them below with the verse numbers where you found them.

1)

2)

3)

4)

NOTES

8. Outline of the book of Hosea

A. The Unfaithfulness Shown to Hosea by Gomer *(1:1-3:5)*.
- Hosea Marries Gomer *(1:1-2:1)*.
- Gomer Commits Adultery *(2:2-23)*.
- Hosea Restores Gomer *(3:1-5)*.

B. The Unfaithfulness Shown to God by Israel *(4:1-14:9)*.
- Israel Commits Adultery *(4:1-6:3)*.
- No Repentance in Israel *(6:4-8:14)*.
- God Judges Israel *(9:1-10:15)*.
- God Restores Israel *(11:1-14:9)*.

Chapter 29
Joel

1. Introduction and Title

A. Joel is a short book with a clear message of warning for God's people. Joel uses a recent plague of locusts to illustrate what the coming judgment of God against Judah will be like. Joel also calls God's people to repent, and offers hope in the day of salvation that follows judgment.

B. The book of Joel takes its name from the prophet Joel, whose name means *Yahweh is God*.

2. Authorship and Date

A. In its opening verse, the book of Joel names the prophet Joel as its author.

B. Although there is discussion over the date for Joel, tradition says that it was written around 835 BC.

3. Purpose, Themes & Structure

A. The dual purpose of the book of Joel is to call the nation of Judah to repentance *(2:1-3:17)*, and to comfort the faithful with the covenant promises of salvation *(3:18-21)*.

B. The theme of Joel is the coming Day of the Lord.

C. Joel is structured to show God's judgment through the Day of the Lord in the past *(1:1-20)*, and the coming Day of the Lord *(2-3)*.

4. Historical Background

Tradition has placed the book of Joel at 835 BC. The book has no mention of a king associated with it. In 835 BC, seven-year-old Joash was placed on the throne in Judah. In Joash's early days, Jehoiada the priest was making the decisions for Joash. Judah itself was not consistent in obeying the covenant with God. Although Joash became a righteous king, rulers before and after him followed their own path. Joel's warnings were needed.

5. Development of Message

Joel develops the theme of the coming Day of the Lord with a series of pronouncements *(1:15; 2:1-2, 11, 31; 3:14, 18)*. Each pronouncement builds on the one before. Promises of future salvation are also part of the book *(2:18-32; 3:17-21)*.

NOTES

6. Theology[26]

A. The Day of the Lord can tell about an event in history, or the judgment of God at the end of history. Three things are often a part of the <u>Day of the Lord</u>:
- The judgment of God's people *(Amo. 5:18-20; Lam. 1:12; Eze. 13:5; Zep. 1:18)*.
- The judgment of foreign nations *(Isa. 13:6, 9; Jer. 46:10; Eze. 39:8)*.
- Israel's purification and restoration *(Isa. 61:2; Mal. 4:5)*, through suffering *(Zec. 14:1-3)*.

B. In the second and third chapters, Joel tells about the future <u>Day of the Lord</u> when God will destroy His enemies and save Israel.

7. Uniqueness and How to Preach It in Your Church Plant

Joel shows how God can use a terrible event like a locust plague to turn people toward Him *(2:12-14)*. It is the same today as it was in Joel's time. Preach that God can use terrible events like a flood, famine, illness, or death to turn a person toward Him *(2 Kings 5:1-16; Mar. 5:21-43)*. Remind people that God can make all things work together for good for those who love Him and are called according to his purposes *(Rom. 8:28)*. No circumstance or person, no matter how terrible, can separate us from God's love through Jesus Christ *(Rom. 8:35-39)*.

Assignment:

Find three ways the Day of the Lord in *Joel 1:1-20* is like the Day of the Lord in *Joel 2:1-11*.

1)

2)

3)

8. Outline of the book of Joel

A. The Day of the Lord Has Come *(1:1-20)*.
- Judgment through Locusts *(1:1-12)*.
- Judgment through Drought *(1:13-20)*.

B. The Day of the Lord is Coming *(2:1-3:21)*.
- The Lord's Army *(2:1-11)*.
- Call to Repent *(2:12-17)*.
- Forgiveness, Restoration, and Deliverance *(2:18-32)*.
- God Judges the Nations *(3:1-16)*.
- Israel is Restored *(3:17-21)*.

Chapter 30
Amos

1. Introduction and Title

A. The book of Amos tells about the ministry of Amos, a shepherd from Judah who prophesied against the injustice and self-centered wealth in the northern kingdom of Israel. Amos spoke that God's judgment was coming because the poor in Israel were ignored and mistreated (even sold into slavery) by those who lived for pleasure.

B. Amos is named for the prophet Amos, whose name means *Burden-bearer*.

2. Authorship and Date

A. The book of Amos states that Amos is its author *(Amos 1:1)*.

B. The book of Amos says that Amos prophesied during the time of Uzziah in Judah (767-739 BC), and Jeroboam II in Israel (782-753 BC). They reigned at the same time during the years of 767-753 BC. Some content in Amos is probably from the later years of Jeroboam *(7:9-11)*. The book of Amos, then, was probably completed sometime from 760-753 BC.

3. Purpose, Themes & Structure

A. The purpose of the book of Amos was to call the leaders in Israel to repent and change their behavior toward the poor. Otherwise, God's judgment would come.

B. The main theme in Amos is God's call to justice. God was angry that people forgot their need to treat others according to their covenant with Him. If God was righteous and just, His people needed to be righteous and just.

C. Amos is structured as a series of messages on judgment.
- Amos begins with eight declarations of judgment on Israel and seven other nations *(1-2)*.
- Amos then brings messages about Israel's past, present and future judgment *(3-6)*.
- Amos then records five symbolic visions of judgment *(7:1-9:10)*.
- The book ends with the promise of Israel's restoration after judgment *(9:11-15)*.

4. Historical Background

Judah and Israel were in times of prosperity when Amos prophesied (around 762-753 BC). Both King Uzziah of Judah and King Jeroboam II of Israel had led their nations into some success and national wealth. In doing so, they had treated the poor without justice. They had thrown the working poor out of their land. Businesses charged the poor unfair prices and interest. God called Amos to speak to the kings and leaders of His people to change their ways, or face His judgment.

5. Development of Message

The message in the book of Amos is of God's coming judgment towards Israel, Judah, and the nations that were in rebellion against Him *(1:1-2:16)*. Their rebellion against God showed in the ways they mistreated the poor and sought pleasure *(2:6-8; 4:1-3)*. Judgment was coming unless they repented *(3:1-9:10)*. After the judgment, God would restore Israel according to His covenant *(9:11-15)*.

6. Theology

Amos tells about God's righteousness and justice *(5:21-24)*. It also says that God requires His people to practice righteousness and justice. If they do not, God will bring judgment upon them *(8:4-10)*. Here, as throughout the Bible, God requires that His character be reflected in His people *(Lev. 11:45; 1 Pet. 1:15-16)*.

7. Uniqueness and How to Preach It in Your Church Plant

Amos tells about a simple shepherd with a big message to deliver *(7:14-15)*. Amos was the first to say that he was not a prophet to earn money. He was a prophet only because God told him to prophesy. Preach that God can use anyone to speak His message. He used a servant girl to speak to an army commander *(2 Kin. 5:1-3)*. He used a child to speak to a high priest *(1 Sam. 3:10-18)*. He used a woman who was disliked in her town to tell them about Jesus *(Joh. 4:28-30, 39-42)*. In the same way, we need to be ready to speak God's message *(1 Pet. 3:15; 2 Tim. 4:2)*.

Assignment:

Find five places in the book of Amos where it says the people of Israel or Judah have mistreated the poor.

1)

2)

3)

4)

5)

8. Outline of the book of Amos

A. Judgment against Israel and the Nations *(1:1-2:16)*.

B. Reasons for Israel's Judgment *(3:1-6:14)*.

C. Visions of Judgment *(7:1-9:10)*.

D. Israel Restored *(9:11-15)*.

Chapter 31
Obadiah

1. Introduction and Title

A. The book of Obadiah tells about the ongoing struggle between Edom and the people of Israel. The Edomites were from the family line of Esau, Jacob's brother. Edom and Israel were usually in some kind of fight with each other. Obadiah says that Edom would be completely destroyed because it always chose to stand against God's chosen people.

B. The book of Obadiah takes its name from the prophet Obadiah, whose name means *Servant of the Lord*.

2. Authorship and Date

A. The book of Obadiah says it contains the words of Obadiah. Nothing is really known about Obadiah's life apart from the words in this book.

B. The struggle with Edom described in Obadiah fits two places in history. One is the revolt of Edom against Judah around 850 BC. The other is when Edom helped Babylon capture Jerusalem in 586 BC. The date of Obadiah's writing, then is either around 850 BC or just after 586 BC.

3. Purpose, Themes & Structure

A. The purpose of Obadiah is to say that God rules over all nations, whether they honor Him or not. This truth provided comfort to the faithful as it reminded them that God had not abandoned them.

B. Obadiah expresses a very strong statement of judgment, and that is the theme of the book. God will completely destroy Edom, and restore Judah.

C. Obadiah is structured in two parts, similar to other short prophetic books.
   • The first part tells about judgment (of Edom) *(1:1-18)*.
   • The second tells about Israel's restoration *(1:19-21)*.

4. Historical Background

Obadiah tells about Edom's actions against Judah. Edom was in a constant struggle against Judah. Around 850 BC, Edom revolted against Judah while the Philistines and Arabians were invading Judah *(2 Chr. 21:8-10, 16-17)*. In 586 BC, Edom may have cooperated with Babylon in the taking of Judah *(Psa. 137:7)*. In either case, history shows that Edom had no desire to be a friend to Judah.

5. Development of Message

The message of Obadiah develops in 21 verses. Edom's judgment is predicted *(1:1-9)*. God's judgment on Edom is then justified, and the results of that judgment are revealed *(1:10-18)*. After the judgment of Edom, Israel is restored *(1:19-21)*.

6. Theology

Obadiah shows that God is the God of every nation. He has the power to place and influence nations in the history of the world *(1:1-4)*. God's judgment in the day of the Lord will fall on all the nations, not just Israel, Judah, and Edom *(1:15-16)*.

7. Uniqueness and How to Preach It in Your Church Plant

The book of Obadiah also tells about the family ties between Edom and Judah. Edom was a part of Esau's family line, and Israel and Judah were part of Jacob's. God judged Edom because Edom harmed Judah *(1:10-11)*. The Bible speaks of other struggles within families *(Gen. 4:1-26; 37:1-36)*. Preach that God's people must learn how to get along with their families *(Eph. 5:22-6:4)*. Family members need to care for one another *(1 Tim. 5:4, 8)*.

Assignment:

Find three of God's reasons for bringing judgment on Edom in the book of Obadiah.

1)

2)

3)

8. Outline of the book of Obadiah

    A. Edom's Coming Destruction *(1:1-9)*.

    B. Edom's Crimes *(1:10-14)*.

    C. God Judges Israel's Enemies *(1:15-16)*.

    D. God Blesses Israel's People *(1:17-21)*.

Chapter 32
Jonah

1. Introduction and Title

A. The book of Jonah tells about the disobedient prophet Jonah and his mission to Nineveh. Jonah shows that God's reach of mercy goes beyond His chosen people into the entire world. It also shows that God's people need to be careful not to think they are better than others.

B. The book of Jonah is named for the prophet Jonah, whose name means *Dove*. Dove may refer either to peace or folly.[27] Either word can fit the story of Jonah.

2. Authorship and Date

A. Jewish tradition says that the book of Jonah was written by Jonah.

B. The book of Jonah was probably written shortly after Nineveh's repentance (about 760 BC).

3. Purpose, Themes & Structure

A. The purpose of Jonah is to show that God is free to demonstrate love and mercy to whomever He pleases.

B. The chief theme of the book is that God rules over all nations. It also shows that God rules over nature, and that His mercy reaches beyond those of us who already know Him. The importance of obedience to God's call on our life is another clear message of Jonah.

C. The book of Jonah is the only prophetic book of the Bible without prophecies. It is structured as a story, with a section that is like a psalm *(2:2-9)*.

4. Historical Background

A. Jonah is spoken of in *2 Kings 14:25*, which tells that Jonah was the son of Amittai *(Jon. 1:1)*. It also says that Jonah was from Gath Hepher, which places Jonah in the northern kingdom of Israel. Jonah's ministry was during the reign of Jeroboam II (about 792-753 BC).

B. This was a time of both prosperity and great disobedience in Israel. It is likely Nineveh was meant to be a lesson for Israel. Nineveh was known for its great violence and cruelty. If Nineveh could repent, Israel had no excuse not to repent.

NOTES

5. Development of Message

The message in the book of Jonah develops with the journey of the prophet to Nineveh. Each stage shows a different part of Jonah's character. Jonah disobeys God by traveling to Tarshish instead of Nineveh. Yet, the sailors on the ship honor God *(1)*. God corrects Jonah's disobedience through a great fish *(2)*. Jonah reaches Nineveh to find the people there ready to receive God's mercy. In contrast, Jonah had hoped they would reject God and be destroyed *(3:1-4:3)*. Finally, God reminds Jonah of His mercy that goes beyond what Jonah wanted *(4:4-11)*.

6. Theology

Jonah shows that God rules over everything. God has power over nature *(1:4-17; 2:10; 4:5-9)*. His mercy changes the hearts and behavior of the nations *(3:5-10)*. His concern is for all His creation *(4:10-11)*.

7. Uniqueness and How to Preach It in Your Church Plant

The book of Jonah shows that God is ready to extend His mercy and grace beyond what is sometimes expected. It seems that Jonah didn't expect God's grace to reach the Ninevites *(3:5-10)*. This is completely consistent with God's character. Preach that God's grace through Jesus Christ extends beyond what we expect. It extended beyond the Jews to a centurion *(Luk. 7:1-10)*. It extended past Simon the Pharisee to a woman who washed Jesus' feet *(Luk. 7:36-49)*. It went beyond an obedient older brother to a disobedient younger brother *(Luk. 15:11-32)*. It even went beyond the righteous to sinners like us *(1 Tim. 1:15)*.

Assignment:

Find three places in the book of Jonah where God shows mercy.

1)

2)

3)

8. Outline of the book of Jonah

A. Jonah's Disobedience *(1:1-2:10)*.
- Jonah and the Great Storm *(1:1-16)*.
- Jonah and the Great Fish *(1:17-2:10)*.

B. Jonah in Nineveh *(3:1-4:11)*.
- Jonah Obeys *(3:1-4)*.
- Nineveh Repents *(3:5-10)*.
- Jonah's Anger *(4:1-3)*.
- God's Response *(4:4-11)*.

NOTES

Chapter 33
Micah

1. Introduction and Title

A. The book of Micah says that God will bring judgment on anyone who mistreats others for personal gain. Micah calls God's people in both the northern and southern kingdoms to remember they needed to live by His covenant to stay in a right relationship with him. If they did not, they would be judged.

B. The book of Micah is named for the prophet Micah, whose name means *Who is like the Lord?*

2. Authorship and Date

A. The book of Micah was written by the prophet Micah.

B. Micah probably compiled this book during his preaching career (about 735-710 BC).

3. Purpose, Themes & Structure

A. The purpose of the book of Micah is to show that personal righteousness is part of keeping God's covenant.

B. Several themes are woven into the book of Micah. One is that God's judgment is certain *(1:2-3:12)*. God expected standards of behavior that fulfilled His laws *(6:6-8)*. The people of Israel and Judah did not care about God's standards. They made up ways to take what others had *(2:1-2)*. The rulers led the way into injustice *(3; 7:2-4)*. Yet after judgment, God would restore His people *(4)*, under the leadership of the Messiah *(5:2-4)*.

C. Micah is structured to leave its hearers ready to repent. It begins with a prophecy of judgment *(1-3)*. It continues, but does not conclude, with a promise of restoration *(4-5)*. It finishes with God asking His people to repent, with salvation to follow *(6-7)*.

4. Historical Background

A. *Micah 1:1* says that Micah prophesied during the time of three kings of Judah: Jotham (739-731 BC), Ahaz (731-715 BC), and Hezekiah (715-686 BC). Micah's prophecies regarding the northern kingdom of Israel and its fall to Assyria place the beginning of his prophetic ministry several years before 722 BC. His prophecies against idolatry in Judah seem to put his ministry at an end before the religious reforms of Hezekiah (about 710 BC). These facts indicate that the ministry of Micah took place from about 735 BC to 710 BC.

B. Micah prophesied at roughly the same time as Hosea, Amos, Isaiah, and Jonah.

5. Development of Message

The message of Micah begins with judgment on the rulers and people of Israel and Judah *(1-3)*. From there, restoration is promised through God's discipline on His people *(4-5)*. Based on the promise of restoration, God asks His people to repent *(6-7)*.

6. Theology

Micah shows that God is far more interested in obedience to His covenant and justice toward others than in legalistic rituals *(6:6-8)*. When God restores His covenant people, He will create a new society that truly follows Him in everyday life *(4:1-8)*.

7. Uniqueness and How to Preach It in Your Church Plant

Micah has one of the clearest prophecies about Jesus Christ in the Old Testament. *Micah 5:2* states that the Messiah would be born in Bethlehem. Several other prophecies in Micah tell about the rule of Jesus Christ over the whole world *(2:12-13; 4:1-5; 5:4-5; Isa. 49:7-13)*. His kingship is marked by power, but also by care and comfort for His people *(Mic. 4:6-8)*. Preach that we can show the rule of Jesus Christ today by having His mind about servanthood *(Phi. 2:5-11)*. Preach that people can see the rule of Jesus Christ if He rules our hearts and minds *(Col. 3:15; 2 Cor. 10:3-5)*. Preach that He is coming again to rule on this earth *(Rev. 4-22.)*

Assignment:

Read *Micah 2:12-13; 4:1-8; 5:4-5*. From these verses, write three things that result from living under the rule of Jesus Christ.

1)

2)

3)

NOTES

NOTES

8. Outline of the book of Micah

    A. God's Judgment on Judah and Israel (Samaria) Prophesied *(1:1-3:12)*.
- The People Judged *(1:1-2:13)*.
- The Leaders Judged *(3:1-12)*.

    B. The Restoration Promised *(4:1-5:15)*.
- Zion's Future *(4:1-5:1)*.
- The Coming Messiah *(5:2-15)*.

    C. God's Call to Repent *(6:1-7:6)*.

    D. Forgiveness and Salvation *(7:7-20)*.

Chapter 34
Nahum

1. Introduction and Title

   A. The book of Nahum tells about God's judgment on Nineveh, the Assyrian capital that had repented after hearing God's warnings through the prophet Jonah. God's prophet Nahum says that because Nineveh failed to continue in obedience to God, they will be destroyed by Babylon.

   B. The book of Nahum takes its name from the prophet Nahum, whose name means *Comfort*.

2. Authorship and Date

   A. The prophet Nahum wrote the book of Nahum. Nahum was a prophet from the southern kingdom of Judah. He was active in the seventh century BC.

   B. Nahum predicts the fall of Nineveh (612 BC). The book also tells about the fall of the Egyptian city Thebes in 663 BC as though it had already happened *(3:8;* Nahum called Thebes *"No Amon")*. Yet, Nahum says nothing about Thebes becoming free again in 654 BC. This places the date for the writing of the book of Nahum between 663 and 654 BC.

3. Purpose, Themes & Structure

   A. God had used Nineveh (the capital of Assyria), as His tool of judgment to bring down the northern kingdom of Israel in 722 BC. The purpose of Nahum is to show that even if God uses a nation or person for His own purposes, that nation or person is still accountable to God to obey His will and ways.[28]

   B. The main theme in Nahum is the coming destruction of Nineveh for its wickedness. A second theme is the comfort of Judah that will result from Nineveh's fall.

   C. The book of Nahum uses questions *(1:6, 9)* to help people think through its content, which has three main sections.
   - The first section announces that Nineveh will be destroyed, and because of that Judah will be comforted.
   - The second section is a prophecy that tells about Nineveh's destruction.
   - The third section tells about the reasons for Nineveh's destruction.

4. Historical Background

   Nineveh, the capital city of Assyria, had repented when it heard God's warning through the prophet Jonah (around 760 BC). But it had fallen back into a pattern of great violence and idolatry by the time of the prophet Nahum (around 660

NOTES

BC). Once the most powerful city in the region, Nineveh was failing. Nahum delivered God's message that because of its great evil, Nineveh would be destroyed. Nineveh's fall to Babylon took place in 612 B.C.

5. Development of Message

The message of the book of Nahum is centered on the destruction of Nineveh. The message begins with a review of God's judgment and righteousness *(1)*. It is developed with a prophecy that gives details of Nineveh's destruction *(2)*. It finishes by telling the reasons for Nineveh's destruction *(3)*.

6. Theology

Nahum tells about God's goodness in His final destruction of a city that is determined to mistreat His people and neglect His ways *(1:7-8)*. At the same time, Judah is encouraged to live in righteousness *(1:15)*. God's people are once again promised restoration *(2:2)*. God will keep His covenant promises by removing threats to His people.

7. Uniqueness and How to Preach It in Your Church Plant

The book of Nahum gives an important lesson: everyone is responsible to live according to God's ways. Even if someone has been used as God's instrument in the past, we need to live in obedience to God today. Preach that we need to keep God's standards each day, as did the apostle Paul *(1 Cor. 9:24-27)*. Say that if we belong to God we must obey Him, no matter what our age or place in life. We cannot let the fact that we served God in the past take the place of serving God today. Compare the examples of young Samuel and Eli's sons in *1 Samuel 2:12-4:21*. Obedience to God is not about ritual or legalism. Obedience is a very tangible way that we can show our love and devotion to Him.

Assignment:

Find four questions God asks in the book of Nahum. Write the questions and their verse numbers in the spaces below.

1)

2)

3)

4)

8. Outline of the book of Nahum

   A. God's Judgment on Nineveh is Guaranteed *(1:1-15)*.
      - Divine Judgment in Action *(1:1-8)*.
      - Nineveh's Destruction Means Judah's Deliverance *(1:9-15)*.

   B. Prophecy of Nineveh's Destruction *(2:1-13)*.

   C. Reasons for Nineveh's Destruction *(3:1-19)*.

NOTES

Chapter 35
Habakkuk

1. Introduction and Title

The book of Habakkuk tells about the days in Judah just before Babylon took the first group of exiles from Judah to Babylon. The book tells about the prophet Habakkuk's struggle with his own faith as he tries to understand how God could use a nation like Babylon to discipline His people. God's answers to Habakkuk's questions produced a greater faith in the prophet, and gave hope to His people.

2. Authorship and Date

A. The prophet Habakkuk wrote the book of Habakkuk. Habakkuk means *Embrace*.

B. Scholars believe the book of Habakkuk was written between the death of King Josiah (609 BC), and the first Babylonian captivity (605 BC).

3. Purpose, Themes & Structure

A. The purpose of the book of Habakkuk is to show that even when it seems that evil is powerful, God is all powerful and will judge evil.

B. Habakkuk has several themes:
- One theme is that although evil and unjust people may seem to be successful *(1:2-4)*, God will judge them *(2:6-20)*.
- Another theme is the struggle of personal faith, especially when things do not make sense *(1:12-2:1; 3:17-19)*.
- A third is the certain punishment of the wicked *(2:5-20)*.

C. The book of Habakkuk is structured like the poetry of Job and the Psalms. In fact, *Habakkuk 3:19* ends the book with the note: *To the Chief Musician. With my stringed instruments.* The book follows a question/answer format. Habakkuk asks the questions and God responds *(1-2)*. It closes with a prayer and hymn of praise *(3)*.

4. Historical Background

A. The book of Habakkuk probably takes place shortly after the death of King Josiah (609 BC), in the early days of the wicked King Jehoiakim's rule in Judah (609-597 BC). Judah was in open rebellion against God. Habakkuk prophesied about God's judgment of Judah through Babylon. He warned that the judgment would follow quickly (as it did in 605 BC when Nebuchadnezzar of Babylon deported 10,000 leaders and citizens from Jerusalem to Babylon).

B. Habakkuk was active at the same time as the prophets Zephaniah and Jeremiah.

5. Development of Message

The message of Habakkuk begins with doubt and confusion *(1:12-2:1)*. God brings clear answers to respond to that doubt *(2:2-20)*. The key to understanding the ways of God is to know that the just live by faith *(2:4)*. God's people have to depend on God, not their own understanding.

6. Theology

Habakkuk deals with the hard question of why wicked people sometimes gain power and success *(1:2-4)*. God has not left His position as Ruler of the universe when this happens. He is ready to judge those who commit evil *(1:5-11; 2:1-4)*. Habakkuk tells that God will wipe out perversion, idolatry and injustice (2:5-19). People with faith in God will be saved *(3:17-19)*.

7. Uniqueness and How to Preach It in Your Church Plant

Sometimes people think that questions and doubts are sins. Habakkuk shows that questions and doubts are not a problem as long as we keep faith in God *(2:4)*. Preach that we do not always understand life, but we do know that God is faithful to us *(2 Tim. 1:12)*. We may face challenges and trials we cannot figure out. Yet no matter what surrounds us, we can be confident that God will reward our faith in Him and obedience to His will *(Heb. 10:35-39)*.

Assignment:

Read *Habakkuk 2:5-20*. In these verses, find three reasons God was bringing judgment on Judah and write them in the spaces below. Write the verse numbers next to the reasons you find.

1)

2)

3)

NOTES

8. Outline of the book of Habakkuk

A. Habakkuk's Questions, God's Replies *(1:1-2:20)*.
   - The First Question and Reply *(1:1-11)*.
   - The Second Question and Reply *(1:12-2:20)*.

B. Habakkuk's Praise *(3:1-19)*.
   - Prayer for Mercy *(3:1-15)*.
   - Hymn of Faith *(3:16-19)*.

Chapter 36
Zephaniah

1. Introduction and Title

A. Zephaniah tells about the day of the Lord, when God will judge the sin of Judah and the surrounding nations. Zephaniah's prophecies made it clear that God's wrath was coming, and calls for God's people to repent. Their response would decide how soon God's judgment would come upon Judah.

B. The book of Zephaniah is named for the prophet Zephaniah, whose name means *The Lord has hidden* or *The Lord treasured*.

2. Authorship and Date

A. Tradition and scholars agree that the prophet Zephaniah wrote the book of Zephaniah.

B. The opening verse of the book of Zephaniah sets the time of Zephaniah's ministry during the reign of King Josiah of Judah (640-609 BC). *Zephaniah 2:13* puts the destruction of Nineveh (612 BC), in the future. It also seems that Zephaniah's lists of Judah's sins *(1:3-13; 3:1-7)* are connected to the time shortly after Josiah's religious reforms (around 622 BC). This puts the writing of the book of Zephaniah sometime between 622 BC and 612 BC.[29]

3. Purpose, Themes & Structure

A. The purpose of Zephaniah is to announce the coming day of the Lord because of God's judgment on the sin of Judah and the nations around it.

B. The themes of Zephaniah contrast God's wrath with His mercy. The opening theme is judgment in the day of the Lord *(1:1-3:8)*. The theme that follows is salvation and restoration in the day of the Lord *(3:9-20)*.

C. The structure of the book of Zephaniah is similar to other prophetic books, especially the book of Joel. Its literary style is similar, as is its message of judgment followed by salvation and restoration for God's faithful followers.

4. Historical Background

A. Zephaniah prophesied during the time of Josiah in Judah (640-609 BC). The prophet lived in Jerusalem and used the religious reforms of Josiah around 622 BC to his advantage. The prophet frequently quoted the Law, which points to his use of the books discovered by Hilkiah. Zephaniah warned those in Judah who had rejected Josiah's reforms to turn back to God or face judgment.

B. Zephaniah was a great-great-grandson of Hezekiah, and so a distant relative to the royalty of Judah he addressed.

NOTES

5. Development of Message

Zephaniah clearly says that the day of the Lord is coming. God's judgment on this day covers not just Jerusalem *(3:1-7)* and Judah *(1:4-2:3)*, but also the nations around Judah *(2:4-15)*, and the whole earth *(1:1-3; 3:8)*. Out of this complete destruction will come restoration and hope for God's people as history ends *(3:9-20)*.

6. Theology

The theology of Zephaniah tells of God's rule over the earth and the nations. It calls God's people to honor and revere Him again with the message, *"Be silent in the presence of the Lord God; for the day of the Lord is at hand" (1:7a)*. God keeps His promise to protect His people, even though judgment is certain *(3:13-17)*.

7. Uniqueness and How to Preach It in Your Church Plant

Zephaniah tells a difficult truth about Judah. Judah's idolatry and immorality had become so great that Judah, God's covenant people, were included in the same sweeping judgment as the Gentile nations around them *(1:1-3:8)*. God expects His people, then and now, to be different than everyone else. Preach that God's people need to think and act like people devoted to Him *(Rom. 12:1-2)*. Preach that Jesus expects a different and higher standard of life from His disciples *(Mat. 5:13-48)*. God's people are to be holy as He is holy *(1 Pet. 1:15-16)*.

Assignment:

Read Zephaniah 3:8-20. In these verses, find three promises of comfort for God's faithful followers. Write the promises next to their verse numbers in the spaces below.

1)

2)

3)

8. Outline of the book of Zephaniah

A. The Day of the Lord: Judgment *(1:1-3:8)*.
- Judgment on All the Earth *(1:1-3)*.
- Judgment on Judah and Jerusalem *(1:4-2:3)*.
- Judgment on the Nations Surrounding Judah *(2:4-15)*.
- Judgment on Jerusalem *(3:1-7)*.
- Judgment on All the Earth *(3:8)*.

B. The Day of the Lord: Restoration *(3:9-20)*.
- The Nations Restored *(3:9-10)*.
- Israel Restored *(3:11-20)*.

Chapter 37
Haggai

1. **Introduction and Title**

    A. The book of Haggai is a collection of four short messages to encourage the Jews in Jerusalem to complete the rebuilding of the temple. The exiles had returned from Babylon with every intention of rebuilding and restoring the temple. Over time their enthusiasm for the temple was lost. They spent more time decorating their homes than rebuilding God's house. Yet they could not receive the fullness of God's blessing until the temple was finished.

    B. The book of Haggai is named for Haggai the prophet, whose name means *Festive* or *Festival*.

2. **Authorship and Date**

    A. Tradition and scholars say that Haggai the prophet is the author of the book of Haggai.

    B. The book of Haggai precisely dates itself as being delivered from 1 September, through 24 December, 520 BC.

3. **Purpose, Themes & Structure**

    A. The purpose of Haggai is to encourage the Jews who had returned from exile in Babylon to rebuild the temple in Jerusalem with a willing heart.

    B. The main theme in Haggai is that if the people of Jerusalem ignored the need to rebuild the temple, they were also ignoring their need to rebuild their hearts.

    C. Haggai is structured in four short messages:
    - The first tells about the connection between the unfinished temple and the difficulties God's people were facing in everyday life *(1:1-15)*.
    - The second says the temple God's people are rebuilding is not as glorious as the first, but will be more glorious than the first if they finish their task *(2:1-9)*.
    - The third says obedience will solve their problems *(2:10-19)*.
    - The fourth tells about God blessing the exiles through final judgment on the nations and the leadership of their governor Zerubbabel *(2:20-23)*.

4. **Historical Background**

    Cyrus of Persia issued a decree in 538 BC that allowed the Jews in exile to return to Palestine and rebuild their temple. Work on the temple began in 536 BC, but opposition from the Samaritans and later the Persians caused the work to stop in 534 BC. Darius removed any Persian resistance by decree in the second year of his reign (520 BC). Haggai the prophet had returned from Babylon with Zerubbabel in 538 BC. God called Haggai (and the prophet Zechariah), to encourage the exiles to complete the temple. Their ministry was effective. Work on the temple began again as a result of Haggai's messages, and was completed four years later (around 516 BC).

5. Development of Message

A. The overall message in Haggai develops as the four messages build on each other.
- First, God calls His people to take responsibility for the condition of the temple. The people's obedience led to God promising that He was with them *(1:13)*.
- Second, God said that the temple His people were rebuilding would be more glorious than the first temple *(2:1-9)*.
- Third, God promises blessing from that day forward *(2:10-19)*.
- The final message says that God would bless His people in the days to come *(2:20-23)*.

B. These messages told God's people that their work on the temple was both pleasing to God's heart and a source of great blessing for them.

6. Theology

Haggai begins with a challenge similar to what Joshua gave Israel: to choose who they would serve *(Hag. 1:3-8; Jos. 24:14-15)*. The Jews in Jerusalem had to make God and His desires their first priority again. Haggai shows that God is a jealous God, just as He had told Moses *(Ex. 20:3-6)*. In God's covenant relationship, He expects His people to choose Him over everything else.

7. Uniqueness and How to Preach It in Your Church Plant

There were many times in the history of God's people where they worshiped idols made of wood, silver or gold. But the book of Haggai tells that God's people were worshiping their own comfort more than they worshiped God *(Hag. 1:3-11)*. It was a different kind of idol, but just as deadly. It is the kind of idol many people worship today. Preach that God's people must make God and His concerns their highest priority *(Mat. 6:24)*. When we make that choice, He will provide everything we need and more *(Mat. 6:31-33)*.

NOTES

Assignment:

In the book of Haggai, find three promises God makes to His people for their obedience in rebuilding the temple. Write the promises and their verse numbers below.

1)

2)

3)

8. Outline of the book of Haggai[30]

    A. Haggai's First Message: Rebuild the Temple *(1:1-15)*.
- God's People Put Off Rebuilding the Temple *(1:1-6)*.
- God Says to Rebuild Now *(1:7-8)*.
- Why the People Suffer *(1:9-11)*.
- The Leaders and People Take Action *(1:12-15)*.

    B. Haggai's Second Message: The Future Temple's Glory *(2:1-9)*.

    C. Haggai's Third Message: The Blessings of Obedience *(2:10-19)*.

    D. Haggai's Fourth Message: Future Blessings *(2:20-23)*.

Chapter 38
Zechariah

1. Introduction and Title

A. Zechariah contains hope and encouragement for the returned Jewish exiles in Jerusalem. The encouragement is for the Jews to complete the rebuilding of the temple. The hope is in the coming Messiah who would bring both salvation and the promised eternal kingdom. Zechariah's words are often quoted in the New Testament because they tell so much about the Messiah, Jesus Christ.

B. The book of Zechariah is named for the prophet Zechariah, whose name means *The Lord Remembers*. It was a great comfort to God's people in Jerusalem that God remembered them and the covenant He had made with them.

2. Authorship and Date

A. Tradition and other scholars say that Zechariah is the author of the book of Zechariah.

B. The first eight chapters of Zechariah are dated from 520-518 BC while the Jews are rebuilding the temple in Jerusalem. *Zechariah 9-14* probably came toward the end of the prophet's ministry between 500 and 470 BC.

3. Purpose, Themes & Structure

A. The purpose of Zechariah was to tell the Jews in Jerusalem to return to God, finish the temple, and to hope in the glorious future God had for them.

B. There are several important themes in Zechariah.
- One is that God had never forgotten His covenant people, or His chosen place for them *(1:12-17)*.
- Another is God's promise to live in and among His people *(2:10-11; 8:3, 23)*.
- Perhaps the most important theme in Zechariah is that God will completely restore His people through the coming Messiah *(9:1-14:21)*.

C. Zechariah is structured using several literary styles. Prophetic messages are common in the book *(1:1-6; 7:1-8)*. Prophetic dreams filled with symbols can be found *(1:7-6:8)*. Two longer prophetic messages called "oracles" make up *Zechariah 9-14*.
- The overall structure begins with a call to repentance *(1:1-6)*. It continues with eight prophetic dreams that tell about blessings for God's repentant people *(1:7-6:8)*. Then Zechariah brings four messages that tell why sincere obedience to God is the best way to keep His covenant *(7-8)*. The book finishes with the prophetic oracles about Israel's future salvation through the work of the Messiah *(9-14)*.

NOTES

4. Historical Background
(see the book of Haggai's Historical Introduction)

Zechariah's references to Greece and some differences in style indicate that Zechariah's later ministry probably took place between 480 and 470 BC. At that time, Xerxes (who made Esther his queen), was king in Persia.

5. Development of Message

The message of the book of Zechariah is developed by taking God's people from repentance *(1:1-6)*, to blessings *(1:7-6:8)*, then to the promise of the Messiah's peace *(6:9-15)*. The next development takes God's people from religious ritual, to obedience *(7:4-14)*, then to the promise of their restoration *(8:1-23)*. The final stage of Zechariah's message development moves God's people from being subject to the Gentile nations *(9:1-8)*, to their being delivered and ruled by the Messiah *(9:9-14:21)*.

6. Theology

The theology of Zechariah features the Person of the Messiah. Selected prophecies from Zechariah, listed in the table below, show how Jesus of Nazareth fulfills them.[31]

Zechariah's Prophecy	*Jesus' Fulfillment*
Messiah enters into Jerusalem on a colt *(Zec. 9:9)*	Mat. 21:4-5 Joh. 12:14-16
Messiah betrayed for 30 pieces of silver *(Zec. 11:12-13)*	Mat. 27:9, 10
Messiah's hands and feet pierced *(Zec. 12:10)*	Joh. 19:37
Messiah's death cleanses from sin *(Zec. 13:1)*	Joh. 1:29 Tit. 3:5
Messiah will reign in new Jerusalem *(Zec. 14:9, 16)*	Rev. 20:4-6
Messiah will serve as Priest-King *(Zec. 6:13)*	Heb. 6:20-7:1
Messiah is God's Shepherd *(Zec. 13:7)*	Joh. 10:11-18

7. Uniqueness and How to Preach It in Your Church Plant

People don't always understand the connections between the Old and New Testaments. It helps when preachers and teachers connect Messianic prophecies in the Old Testament with what the New Testament says about Jesus Christ. In many ways Zechariah confirms that Jesus Christ is the Messiah. So do many other books of the Old Testament. Preach that there are good reasons to believe that Jesus is the Messiah *(1 Cor. 15:3-5)*. Show the connections between Old Testament prophecies and what the New Testament says about Jesus *(Mat. 1:22-23; 2:5-6; 4:13-16; Luk. 4:16-21)*. Give hope that Jesus is coming back to reign here on earth *(Zec. 14:9, 16)*.

> **Assignment:**
>
> Read *Zechariah 9-14*. Find three prophecies about the Messiah's rule over God's people, and write them along with their verse numbers in the spaces below.
>
> 1)
>
> 2)
>
> 3)

8. Outline of the book of Zechariah

- A. Eight Symbolic Visions *(1:1-6:15)*.
  - Introduction: Call to Repent *(1:1-6)*.
  - The Red Horse among the Myrtles *(1:7-17)*.
  - The Four Horns and Four Craftsmen *(1:18-21)*.
  - The Surveyor with the Measuring Line *(2:1-13)*.
  - The Cleansing of Joshua the High Priest *(3:1-10)*.
  - The Gold Lampstand and Two Olive Trees *(4:1-14)*.
  - The Flying Scroll *(5:1-4)*.
  - The Woman in the Basket *(5:5-11)*.
  - The Four Chariots *(6:1-8)*.
  - Conclusion: The Symbolic Crowning of Joshua *(6:9-15)*.

- B. Four Messages *(7:1-8:23)*.
  - Introduction: The Question about Fasting *(7:1-3)*.
  - Message of Rebuke *(7:4-7)*.
  - Message of Repentance *(7:8-14)*.
  - Message of Restoration *(8:1-17)*.
  - Message of Rejoicing *(8:18-23)*.

- C. Two Prophetic Oracles *(9:1-14:21)*.
  - The Anointed King Rejected *(9:1-11:17)*
  - The Rejected King Reigns *(12:1-14:21)*

Chapter 39
Malachi

1. **Introduction and Title**

    A. The book of Malachi shows what happens when God's people both forget His love for them, and live in rebellion. Over seventy years had passed since the second temple in Jerusalem had been dedicated. The temple should have been a place of heartfelt celebration of God's presence among His people. Yet over time, worship in Jerusalem had become empty. The people of God forgot God as they worshiped. As a result, they forgot His ways in everyday life. God called Malachi to declare judgment on His people, and also to call them back to Him.

    B. The book of Malachi is named for the prophet Malachi, whose name means *My Messenger*.

2. **Authorship and Date**

    A. The book of Malachi says that Malachi the prophet was its author.

    B. Malachi's prophetic ministry took place while Persia still had political control over Israel. Malachi says that sacrifices were being offered in the temple, which had been completed in 515 BC. Malachi's messages dealt with many of the same problems as Nehemiah. We can probably date Malachi's ministry and message to the time between 432 and 425 BC. This was a time when Nehemiah was in Persia, and before Nehemiah returned to Jerusalem.

3. **Purpose, Themes & Structure**

    A. The purpose of Malachi is to call God's people to a new commitment and obedience in response to God's covenant.

    B. The themes in Malachi tell about how important a person's heart and attitudes are in true worship. Malachi demands that everyone, from the priests to the people, should test their attitudes toward God and each other. Malachi says that the people do not care about God, and mistreat each other *(2:13-15)*. God's people have forgotten His love for them *(1:2)*.

    C. Malachi is structured in six messages.
    - The first message calls for a response to God's love *(1:1-5)*.
    - The second says that God's people should change their attitude toward God from disrespect to honor *(1:6-2:9)*.
    - The third message calls God's people to be faithful to the covenant *(2:10-16)*.
    - The fourth message tells God's people to put their hope in Him *(2:17-3:6)*.
    - The fifth message calls God's people to obey Him *(3:7-12)*.
    - The sixth message reminds God's people to fear Him *(3:13-4:3)*.

D. Each message begins with a question or a charge. The message that follows answers the question or proves the charge to be true. This is a style that confronts its hearers.

4. Historical Background

A. Persian rule brought a time of peace to Palestine. Persia had allowed the Jews to return to their land. The military power of Persia kept other nations under control at the time Malachi was written. Persia collected taxes, but otherwise left the Jews alone. However, shortages of money and food were common.

B. The turmoil among God's people in Jerusalem at the time of Malachi was internal. People were neglecting worship *(3:13-18)*. Priests were corrupt *(1:6-2:9)*. Tithes and offerings were ignored *(3:7-12)*. God's people married pagan wives *(2:10-12)*. People were unfaithful in their marriages *(2:13-15)*. The people of God could have easily become like the nations around them without God's messenger Malachi.

5. Development of Message

The message of the book of Malachi is like that of many books in the Old Testament: if God's people were to have the blessings of His covenant, they needed to obey His covenant. In this book, God's people need to obey the covenant not just with the right ceremonies, but from their hearts. This is why Malachi asks first that God's people love and honor God with true worship *(1:1-2:9)*. The prophet reminds God's people of their responsibilities under the covenant to be faithful and hope in God alone *(2:10-3:6)*. Finally, Malachi tells God's people to obey and fear God *(3:7-4:3)*.

6. Theology

Malachi shows that God is still the faithful partner in the covenant with His people *(3:1-7)*. Yet, God's people are keeping back their love and obedience, so God is keeping back His blessing *(2:13-14)*. Malachi makes it plain that in the covenant relationship, God is the active partner in restoring the relationship. He is willing to be tested. The "test" cannot be in a way that confronts His authority. The right kind of test is to obey God's commands and see how His blessing follows *(3:10)*.

7. Uniqueness and How to Preach It in Your Church Plant

Malachi shows that the worship of God is not just a matter of the right ceremony or ritual, but even more a matter of the right heart toward God. Malachi makes the point clear that disobedient action stems from a disloyal and unloving heart (see the example of the corrupt priests in *2:1-9*). Preach that love for God is shown through obedience *(Joh. 14:15; 15:10)*. Remind God's people that they show their love for God as they help His people *(Heb. 6:10)*.

> **NOTES**

> **Assignment:**
>
> Read *Malachi 2:10-16*. Find and list three things God says in these verses about having a good marriage and the verse numbers where you found them.
>
> 1)
>
> 2)
>
> 3)

8. Outline for the book of Malachi[32]

   A. Malachi's Burden *(1:1)*.

   B. The First Message: Respond to God's Love *(1:1-5)*.

   C. The Second Message: Honor God *(1:6-2:9)*.

   D. The Third Message: Be Faithful as God's Covenant People *(2:10-16)*.

   E. The Fourth Message: Hope in God *(2:17-3:6)*.

   F. The Fifth Message: Obey God *(3:7-12)*.

   G. The Sixth Message: Fear God *(3:13-4:3)*.

   H. Prepare for God's Coming *(4:4-6)*.

NOTES

Endnotes

1. These descriptions and the section lists of books come from Earl D. Radmacher, Ronald B. Allen & H. Wayne House, *Nelson's New Illustrated Bible Commentary*, (Nashville: Thomas Nelson, 1999), "Divisions and Books of the Old Testament," xxxii.
2. This insight and what follows about the New Testament writers come from Gleason L. Archer, *A Survey of Old Testament Introduction* (Chicago: Moody Press, 1974), 26-27.
3. As stated in the text, these are just a few Messianic prophecies from Isaiah listed in John F. Walvoord & Roy B. Zuck, "Messianic Prophecies in the Book of Isaiah," *The Bible Knowledge Commentary* (Old Testament) (Wheaton: Victor Press, 1985), 1049.
4. "The Old Testament at a Glance," *Nelson's New Illustrated Bible Commentary*, Earl Radmacher, Ronald Allen, H. Wayne House, eds. (Nashville: Thomas Nelson, 1999), xxix.
5. Most dates of writing for this book follow H.L. Willmington, *Willmington's Guide to the Bible* (Wheaton: Tyndale House Publishers, Inc., 1982), 802-803.
6. "The Patriarchs," *Nelson's Commentary*, 27.
7. "Sin Is a Choice," *Nelson's Commentary*, 12.
8. This outline is mostly derived from Gleason Archer, *A Survey of Old Testament Introduction* (Chicago: Moody Press, revised edition, 1974).
9. These are derived from Radmacher, Allen and House, *The Nelson Study Bible* (Nashville: Thomas Nelson, 2007), 159.
10. This list is derived from Walvoord & Zuck, *The Bible Knowledge Commentary* (Wheaton: Victor Books, 1985) 260, and Nelson Study Bible second edition (Nashville: Thomas Nelson, 2007; Earl Radmacher, Ronald Allen, Wayne House, Eds.) 269.
11. Gleason Archer, *A Survey of Old Testament Introduction*, (Chicago: Moody Press, 1974) 258-9.
12. Donald Campbell, "Joshua," *The Bible Knowledge Commentary*, John Walvoord and Roy Zuck, eds. (Wheaton: Victor Books, 1985), 325.
13. See *The Nelson Study Bible*, Radmacher, Allen, and House, eds. (Nashville: Thomas Nelson, 2007), 614.
14. See *The Nelson Study Bible*, Radmacher, Allen, and House, Eds (Nashville: Thomas Nelson, 2007), 660.
15. Revised mostly from *The Nelson Study Bible*, Radmacher, Allen, and House, eds. (Nashville: Thomas Nelson, 2007), 732.
16. Harold L. Willmington, *Willmington's Guide to the Bible* (Wheaton: Tyndale House, 1981) 802.
17. Sid Buzzell, "Proverbs," in *The Bible Knowledge Commentary*, John Walvoord and Roy Zuck, eds. (Wheaton: Victor Books, 1985), 901.
18. *The Nelson Study Bible*, Radmacher, Allen, and House, eds. (Nashville: Thomas Nelson, 2007) 964.
19. *The Nelson Study Bible*, Radmacher, Allen and House, eds., (Nashville: Thomas Nelson, 2007), 1009.
20. *The Nelson Study Bible*, Radmacher, Allen and House, eds., (Nashville: Thomas Nelson, 2007) 1026.
21. The Nelson Study Bible. Radmacher, Allen and House, eds., (Nashville: Thomas Nelson, 2007) 1026.
22. Adapted from Jack Deere, "Song of Songs," *The Bible Knowledge Commentary*, Walvoord and Zuck, eds. (Wheaton: Victor Books, 1985), 1010-1011.
23. John Martin, "Isaiah," in *The Bible Knowledge Commentary*, Walvoord and Zuck, eds., (Wheaton: Victor Books, 1985), 1032.
24. Charles Dyer, "Ezekiel," *The Bible Knowledge Commentary*, Walvoord and Zuck, eds. (Wheaton: Victor Books, 1985), 1226.

Endnotes

[25] Revised from Dyer, *The Bible Knowledge Commentary,* and *The Nelson Study Bible*, Radmacher, Allen and House, eds. (Nashville: Thomas Nelson, 2007).

[26] Robert Chisholm, "Joel," in *The Bible Knowledge Commentary*; Walvoord and Zuck, eds. (Wheaton: Victor Books, 1985) 1412.

[27] *The Nelson Study Bible*, Radmacher, Allen and House eds. (Nashville: Thomas Nelson, 2007) 1409.

[28] *The Nelson Study Bible*, Radmacher, Allen and House, eds. (Nashville: Thomas Nelson, 2007) 1428.

[29] John Hannah, "Zephaniah," in *The Bible Knowledge Commentary*, Walvoord and Zuck, eds. (Wheaton: Victor Books, 1985), 1523.

[30] Revised from F. Duane Lindsey, "Haggai," *The Bible Knowledge Commentary*, Walvoord and Zuck, eds. (Wheaton: Victor Books, 1985), 1538.

[31] Revised from *The Nelson Study Bible,* Radmacher, Allen and House, eds. (Nashville: Thomas Nelson, 2007), 1453-4.

[32] Revised from Craig Blaising, "Malachi," *The Bible Knowledge Commentary*, Walvoord and Zuck, eds. (Wheaton: Victor Books, 1985), 1574-5.

Made in the USA
Columbia, SC
26 May 2018